MODERN ED

MODERN EDUCATIONAL DANCE

Rudolf Laban

Third edition revised with an additional chapter by

Lisa Ullmann

Formerly Director of the Laban Art of Movement Centre

Northcote House

British Library Cataloguing in Publication Data

Laban, Rudolf, *1879-1958*
    Modern educational dance.——3rd ed.
    1. Schools. Curriculum subjects: Modern
    dance — For teaching
    I. Title   II. Ullmann, Lisa, *d.1985*
    793.3'2'071

    ISBN 0-7463-0528-1

First edition 1948, reprinted 1950, 1953, 1955, 1956, 1961.
Second edition 1963, reprinted 1968, 1971, 1973.
Third edition 1975, reprinted 1976, 1980, 1988.

Reprinted in 1988 by Northcote House Publishers Ltd, Harper &
Row House, Estover Road, Plymouth PL6 7PZ, United Kingdom.
Tel: Plymouth (0752) 705251.   Telex: 45635.   Fax: (0752) 777603.

Printed and bound by The Guernsey Press Co. Ltd.,
Guernsey, Channel Islands.

PREFATORY NOTE

THIS book is devised as a guide for teachers and parents. The ideas incorporated in it deal with that branch of the art of movement which in English-speaking countries has been called "Modern Dance". Although this term is misleading, because many people will be inclined to think of ballroom dancing, it has been so widely accepted that its use in the present publication seems justified.

The research and practice of this kind of movement study were started many years ago in Paris by the author, who was born in Czechoslovakia. The original name used for the new kind of dancing was "*la danse libre*" or "free dance". Why this name was chosen will be manifest from the context. The spreading of the work in many countries of the European continent led to the name "Central-European dance", though the same dance forms were initiated simultaneously in America. Europe was, however, the cradle of a comprehensive theory. The prominent representatives of the new dance form on the stage, in recreation and education, and of the application of the newly discovered movement principles in industry, were recruited from many nations all over the globe.

Faced with the task of describing the application of the new dance forms to contemporary school education, the author has had to rely upon the reports of his eminent pupils active in this field. His thanks are due to so many of them that they can only be expressed generally.

Due acknowledgment has, however, to be given to those who helped this publication immediately. Miss Lisa Ullmann contributed notes concerning her widespread activity in British schools and teacher-training. Miss Veronica Tyndale Biscoe helped me to make the text as readable as possible.

The publication has been urged by the directors of the "Modern Dance Holiday Courses", who contributed so much to the spreading of the new dance form in this country.

The conviction that, at an age when the child's natural urge to dance has sufficiently developed, it is possible and of educational value to base dance tuition upon the principles of contemporary movement research might justify the hope that with this guide a useful tool, or at least some stimulus, will be given to educationists and parents interested in the subject.

RUDOLF LABAN.

Manchester.
February 6, 1948.

PREFACE TO SECOND EDITION

In revising this book my main consideration was to preserve the spirit and the original style of it and yet to make the reading a little easier. I have, therefore, refrained from elaborating any aspects and have touched only on those things where I felt the meaning remained obscured by awkward language.

The world of movement which Laban endeavoured to open up to everyone throughout his life is, in its constant flux, a highly interrelated reality and to read about it requires of the reader a similar mobile and relating mind. If I have succeeded in my aim I hope the reader will then find this little book a source of unending inspiration, even more so than hitherto. My particular thanks go to Miss Betty Redfern, who so graciously gave of her time in helping me with this task.

It may interest readers to know that the design on the cover of the book is an illustration of one of Laban's space concepts.

LISA ULLMANN.

Addlestone, Surrey.
August 1963.

PREFACE TO THIRD EDITION

I AM pleased that this new edition gives me the opportunity to add some hints for the student of movement. While there was nothing that I wished to amend in the text, I felt the reader might be interested in some of the considerations which I have in my mind when presenting dance movement to the learner.

It is difficult to give an image of a movement experience by describing the factors which bring it about, but I have tried to refrain from using poetical language. I hope that my small addition to the book, which is derived from my practical work as a teacher, will make the reader even more alert to the importance of absorbing the fundamentals of educational dance as expounded by Laban in his text.

LISA ULLMANN.

Addlestone, Surrey.
May 1974.

PREFACE TO THIRD EDITION REPRINT

When the first edition of MODERN EDUCATIONAL DANCE appeared in 1948 it made a great impression on all groups involved with physical training and education. Physical training, primarily competition-orientated until that time, experienced a wide-ranging expansion as a result of this book into musical-creative areas. In order to reduce the difficulties caused by the decrease in expressive movements during puberty, and self-control over competitive movements found in our advanced society, practice in the physical and mental control of physical movement and the encouragement of creative forms of movement are both necessary even at school.

Rudolf Laban considered both to be a part of MODERN EDUCATIONAL DANCE. For him this was a broad term, covering not only the rudiments of artistic dance and the folk dance but the rudiments of everyday, working and sport movements, too. The circle of people who can make use of this book is correspondingly wide: teachers, psychologists, ergonomics experts, sportsmen and sports teachers, students, dancers and teachers of dance, physiotherapists — in short, all those professions which are based on, use and care for the human body.

Although this book was written for schools at the end of the industrial age, it is gaining in importance for general education in movement in our electronic age. The fact that new editions and reprints of this book have been required again and again, and that it has been translated into several foreign languages, confirms its growing relevance and value today. May this latest edition, too, be a stimulus and a guide to all those committed, open-minded and critical practitioners and researchers in the sphere of education in movement at schools, in the professions, and in leisure activities alike.

ROLAND LABAN

Semriach, Austria,
October 1988.

CONTENTS

	Prefatory Note	v
	Preface to Second Edition	vii
	Preface to Third Edition	viii
	Preface to Third Edition Reprint	ix
I	Introduction	1
II	Dancing throughout the Age Groups	14
III	Sixteen Basic Movement Themes	25
IV	Rudiments of a Free Dance Technique	52
V	The Conception of the Sphere of Movement	85
VI	The Observation of Movement	97
VII	Some Hints for the Student of Movement (*by Lisa Ullmann*)	108
	Index	135

CHAPTER I

INTRODUCTION

IT is more widely realised today that school education must take the subject of dance tuition into consideration. The question which arises is, how shall we proceed? Do the remnants of the historical art of dancing offer a sufficient foundation on which to build the new dance tuition in school, or do we need, in our complex modern civilisation, a new approach to the problem? The answer is, I think, that we must look around us and compare the conditions of life in our time with those of the days in which the traditional dance forms originated.

We should also investigate what connection exists between the dance forms and the general behaviour, especially the working habits, of a particular period. Compared with what is known in this respect concerning the other arts, our knowledge in the field of the art of movement is very scanty.

The history of architecture, sculpture, painting, music, and poetry describes the changes which these arts have undergone in the various epochs and periods of civilisation. The differences between Greek temples, Gothic cathedrals and the skyscrapers of our time are so obvious that everybody can see them clearly. It is easy to awaken an interest in the changes in the social order and life conditions through history and explain how the typical forms of, say, an architectural period are connected with the general trend and character of the public life of that age. Similar connections between social-life forms and the products of all the other arts except that of dance can be easily demonstrated. It is thus that few people think in this connection of dance, the fundamental art of man. Whereas all the other arts have left witnesses in the form of buildings, pictures, manuscripts of poetry and music, the art of movement of past eras has faded away, leaving no traces other than incidental descriptions either in words, which are inadequate to give a picture of movement, or in choreographies which nobody can really decipher.

The tradition of dance practice has kept a few of the dances of more recent periods of civilisation alive. We know some of the medieval folk-dances and the dances of the period of absolute monarchies which preceded the recent political and industrial revolution. Yet the whole inheritance of the art of movement throughout history is so meagre that it has hardly occurred to the great public that there is a connection between the changes of social life and dance. The methodical study of the movement forms contained in dances and of their repercussion upon the various fields of public life has hardly started. The rôle of the art of movement in education has only lately been rediscovered. All we know is that in ancient times dance played a much greater rôle in public life, yet the primitive forms of communal dancing, as still seen today with natives of other continents, are as strange to us as their whole civilisation. They cannot serve either as a model or as a sufficient source of inspiration.

It thus seems that modern man has to create his own art of movement, and a beginning to this can be seen in those dance forms of our time which the Americans and, with them, other English-speaking countries, call "Modern Dance" (see also page v).

Compared with the relics of medieval folk-dances and with the movement forms of the times of absolutist kingdoms, "Modern Dance" is richer and freer in gestures and steps. A second outstanding characteristic of the contemporary art of movement is the correspondence between the new forms of dance expression and the movement habits of modern man. Our time has not inappropriately been called the epoch of industrial revolution, and it might be permissible to call "Modern Dance" the movement expression of industrial man.

Dances have had at all times a profound connection with the working habits of the periods in which they arose or were created. About the middle of the 18th century (1760) a remarkable man, Jean George Noverre, a French ballet-master, turned intuitively away from the Court dances of his time. We can surmise that it was the climate of thought which led to the French Revolution which opened his eyes, though he never tells us whether this was really the case. It might also be that he foresaw the coming development of industrial civilisation, and out of the vision of new, hitherto unseen forms of human working actions he endeavoured to create a new movement expression on the stage. However this may be, Noverre was the first to find both the old peasant dances and the King's amusements unsuitable for the man of the rising industrial centres.

What he did in practice was to abolish the old stage costumes, head-dresses, and decorations which impeded the free flow of movement. He created the "*ballet d'action,*" in which, instead of ceremonious bows and niceties, the full scale of human passions found its expression. But, in my opinion, his greatest deed was that he sent his pupils into the streets, market-places, and workshops in order that they should study the movements of their contemporaries instead of copying the polite behaviour of princes and courtiers. The movements of the latter were without doubt charming and showed great aesthetical perfection. The crux was, however, that they lacked life, or rather the connection with the buzzing life of the cities which were filled with the representatives of a new race, the first forebears of industrial man.

Noverre was an artist, and he worked exclusively for the stage. The description of his ballets and his own writings show, however, that he was a visionary who foretold the spiritual trends of our present time. The curious thing is that he expressed these predictions not in words, but in movements.

Since his time many dancers and producers of ballets have followed his new trend of movement expression, although the dream world of fairies and princes, with their stylised evolutions in space, has continued to attract the public for more than a century.

It was in industry that the new movement research was inaugurated. Since it became obvious that the working processes of a mechanised age are so profoundly different from those of the pre-revolutionary periods of European civilisation, several attempts have been made to adapt the workman's movements to the new needs. A man who must be mentioned in this connection is Frederick W. Taylor, the initiator of the so-called "scientific management." He was one of the first people who tried to penetrate the riddle of human movement from an entirely new point of view. His aim was, of course, to increase the efficiency of workmen operating machines, without ever thinking of the aesthetical values which their movements might have. But he had an inkling of the educational value of movement, especially so far as the education of industrial apprentices was concerned.

A contemporary of Taylor, though without any connection with him, and probably even without knowledge of his industrial endeavours, was Isadora Duncan. She was convinced that the liberation of movement from the fetters of traditional habits could be achieved only by returning to the dance forms of earlier periods of dance history, and especially to the movement forms of Ancient Greece. Taking Greek sculptures and vase-pictures as models, she tried to reconstruct the dance forms of two thousand years ago. Pictures can never give reliable indications of the rhythms and shapes of dance, because they are static images of such stages of the movement as are pictorially interesting. I think that Isadora Duncan's valuable dances were for the most part the expression of our time, and that they had a merely external resemblance to the movement forms of Ancient Greece.

In freeing the dancer's body from excessive clothing, which hinders the flow of movement, she contributed very much to the tendency of contemporary man to overcome his self-consciousness expressed in the hiding of his body. The main achievement of Duncan was, however, that she reawakened a form of dance expression which could be called dance lyrics, in contrast to the mainly dramatic dance forms of the ballet. There was no story behind her dances, which were, as she herself termed it, the expression of the life of her "soul."

She reawakened the sense of the poetry of movement in modern man. At a time when science, and especially psychology, endeavoured to abolish radically any notion of a "soul," this dancer had the courage to demonstrate successfully that there exists in the flow of man's movement some ordering principle which cannot be explained in the usual rationalistic manner. It was especially the influence which the repeated perform- ance of similar movements has on man's internal and external attitude to life which interested her as an educationist.

Movement considered hitherto—at least in our civi- lisation—as the servant of man employed to achieve an extraneous practical purpose was brought to light as an independent power creating states of mind frequently stronger than man's will. This was quite a disconcert- ing discovery at a time when extraneous achievements through will-power seemed to be the paramount objec- tive of human striving.

Industrial movement research has confirmed that this intuitive discovery of the artist is true. We know today that modern working habits frequently create detri- mental states of mind from which our whole civilisation is bound to suffer if no compensation can be found. The most obvious compensations are, of course, those move- ments which are able to counterbalance the disastrous influence of the lopsided movement habits arising in contemporary working methods.

In the pre-industrial epoch of our civilisation crafts- men and peasants had a rich movement-life. In all their occupations the whole body was engaged at various times in the widely different activities which each man had to perform. They had to think, because every man was the organiser of his own business. Procuring raw material, buying, transporting, the productive process itself, and selling, were done by one and the same man. Today's industrial worker is specialised not only in one of these jobs, but in a particular function of a job, frequently in one relatively simple movement sequence which he has to perform from morning till evening throughout his lifetime. He has to think, but within a very restricted sphere of interests. His leisure time is inadequately filled with pleasures lacking that integration of bodily and mental enhancement which in former times arose from pride in work and organisatory independence. The pride in work incidentally found its expression in festive dances. During their school-time children of our day have not learnt to appreciate movement. They hardly know how much their future happiness depends on a rich movement-life.

Education today endeavours to supply a counterbalance to this state of affairs by paying more attention to the arts in general, including the art of movement, since it is realised that dance is the basic art of man.

Dance has today re-entered the realm of the arts, and even the historical forms have regained a new lease of life through the intuitively felt need of almost everybody to obtain, if not inspiration, at least information concerning one of the most powerful features of man's bodily and mental make-up, movement.

In modern educational dance, consideration is given

to all that has been discovered and felt concerning this art by its most prominent pioneers, including those who have studied movement from the more prosaic aspect of working efficiency. This consideration finds its expression in the richness of liberated movement forms, gestures, and steps, as well as in the movements which contemporary man uses in his everyday life.

A new conception of the elements of movement based on modern work research has been introduced into dance tuition. The basic idea of the new dance training is that actions in all kinds of human activities, and therefore also in dance, consist of movement sequences in which a definite effort of the moving person underlies each movement.

The distinction of a specific effort becomes possible because each action consists of a combination of effort elements.* The effort elements derive from attitudes of the moving person towards the motion factors Weight, Space, Time, and Flow. The new dance training fosters the development of a clear and precise awareness of the various efforts in movement, thus guaranteeing the appreciation and enjoyment of any, even the simplest, action movements.

Knowledge of human effort, and especially the efforts used by industrial man, is the basis of the dance tuition applied by many pupils of the author who, becoming teachers or artists, have played a prominent rôle in the development of this contemporary art of movement.

It becomes necessary at this point to clear up a few fundamental conceptions concerning the art of move-

* See R. Laban and F. C. Lawrence, *Effort*, Macdonald & Evans, London, 1974.

ment, which comprises more than dance in its narrower sense.

The art of movement is used on the stage in ballet, pantomime, drama, and in any other kind of performance, including films. All forms of social dancing, country or ballroom dancing and so on, constitute part of the art of movement, as well as a great number of party games, masquerades and many other social plays and entertainments.

The art of movement is implicated in all ceremonies and rituals, and forms part of the speaker's outfit in all kinds of oratory and meetings. Our everyday behaviour is ruled by certain aspects of the art of movement, and so is a great part of the behaviour and activity of children in schools. Games imply the knowledge and experience of the movements used in them, which require a technique of moving. This technique, like that used in the skilled performance of industrial operations, is a part of the art of movement.

The technique of moving has several aspects, one of which is that cultivated in dance tuition.

Traditional dance technique deals with the mastery of individual movements required in particular styles of dancing. The performance of dances is not restricted to the stage. Apart from the theatrical dance compositions of the ballet, each of the social forms of the art of dance, such as national, folk, and ballroom dances, has its own forms of movement and technique.

The new dance technique promoting the mastery of movement in all its bodily and mental aspects is applied in modern dance as a new form of stage dancing and of social dancing. The educational value of this new dance technique can be ascribed to a great extent to the universality of the movement forms which are studied and mastered in the contemporary aspect of this art.

The methodical approach to the universal forms of movement is bound to be different from that needed for the mastery of a particular stylisation of movement embracing only a relatively small section of human movement expression.

One of the most obvious differences between the traditional European dances and modern dance is that the former are almost exclusively step dances, while the latter uses the flow of movement pervading all articulations of the body.

The richness of movement in modern dance demands a different approach for its mastery. It is, indeed, impossible, taking the flow of human movement as a whole, to study the almost infinite variations of steps and bodily carriage in the same manner as can be done with the restricted number of movements used in the stylised dance forms. Instead of studying each particular movement, the principle of moving must be understood and practised. This approach to the material of dancing involves a new conception of it, namely, of movement and its elements.

It is, as we think, mainly the inner attitude mirrored in the new dance technique which makes its application to education desirable and successful.

In olden times dance technique was adapted to the practical needs of performances of dancing, and it is only in our time that certain parts of dance technique have been applied to other fields of human activity. The importance of a new form and spirit of movement education in our time is evident in several respects.

Firstly, the great variety of operations in the more than eighteen thousand occupations of modern man demands the study and mastery of the common denominator of the technical exertions involved in all his working actions. The common denominator is the flow of movement.

Secondly, the unsurpassed amount of intellectual knowledge required for the mastery of modern life needs a balancing factor in which the spontaneous faculties of man can find exercise and outlet. The study and mastery of the spontaneous functions of man which have to be fostered point to the same common denominator, the flow of movement.

The new dance technique offers the possibility of systematically teaching the new movement forms by propounding at the same time their conscious mastery. The industrialists and educationists who have seized the opportunity given by the present-day movement research which the pioneers of modern dance have evolved, have tried to apply the new methods of movement training in factories and schools.

It should be noted that it is not dancing proper which has been applied to these purposes, but the technique used for the movement education of the dancer.

Modern dance as an art has its place on the stage and in recreation. The performance of modern dance compositions, even in the modest form of simple recreational dances, shows a perfection which demands the inspiration of creative and interpretative artists who will not always be available in schools and factories.

In schools where art education is fostered, it is not **artistic perfection** or the creation and performance of sensational dances which is aimed at, but the beneficial effect of the creative activity of dancing upon the personality of the pupil. The question of producing dances in schools must therefore be treated with extreme delicacy and will have to follow definite outlines and procedures which must be discussed in detail. The essential tool which can be offered to the educationist in modern dance is the universal outlook upon the principles of human movement.

The practical use of the new dance technique in education is manifold. The innate urge of children to perform dance-like movements is an unconscious form of outlet and exercise introducing them to the world of the flow of movement, and strengthening their spontaneous faculties of expression. The first task of the school is to foster and to concentrate this urge, and to make the children of the higher age-groups conscious of some of the principles governing movement.

The second and no less important task of education is to preserve the spontaneity of movement and to keep this spontaneity alive up to school-leaving age, and beyond it into adult life.

A third task is the fostering of artistic expression in the medium of the primary art of movement. Here two quite distinct aims will have to be pursued. One is to aid the creative expression of children by producing dances appropriate to their gifts and to the stage of their development. The other is to foster the capacity for taking part in the higher unit of communal dances produced by the teacher.

A further task can be seen in the awakening of a broad outlook on human activities through the observation of the flow of movement used in them.

The terminology, and the inner attitude gained through the assimilation of the new dance technique, can help towards the recognition of one's own and other people's movement deficiencies. The teacher might more easily find the appropriate measures for improving deficient movements, while the pupil will accept his advice more readily and with a better understanding.

Considering the central position of movement in all human activities, many more opportunities of applying the principles of the new dance technique can be imagined and will without doubt emerge from practice.

It should be mentioned finally that the new dance technique endeavours to integrate intellectual knowledge with creative ability, an aim which is of paramount importance in any form of education.

A technique complying with all these requirements necessitates a closer scrutiny of the new outlook upon the child's attitude to dance, and to this we proceed.

CHAPTER II

DANCING THROUGHOUT THE AGE-GROUPS

BEFORE embarking on any system of dance training in schools, it is useful to try to understand the child's instinctive efforts at self-development.

The first efforts of a baby are the stirrings of his body. The baby obviously knows how to set his body-engine into gear, this capacity being a natural gift common to all living beings. What the child learns in his instinctive yet assiduous self-training is not so much an appreciation of movement as the mastery of more and more complicated forms of activity.

The first activity of a baby consists of the moving of his limbs. In pushing his legs away from the centre of the body and in hitting with the arms he loosens the spherical, ball-like position which the body assumed during the embryonic state. This is a natural action which, though instinctively performed, has an obvious aim. Although the aim is not known to the baby, he is driven to perform the action repeatedly until the stretched position of the body becomes as natural to him as the former rolled-up position.

What is interesting to the investigator of dance is the great resemblance of these first stirrings of a human being to the first dancing jump which a child attempts to do a few years later. Primitive dances of adults as still seen today performed by natives of other continents also show the same fundamental movement principle of kicking legs and hitting arms. The difference between a baby's first movements and the dance movements of children who have reached walking stage is that the baby trains a function of the muscular and nervous apparatus, while the dancing child, and so also the primitive adult, wants to overcome gravity in short fits of suspension in the air away from the ground. In other cases, however, one might gain the impression that the dancer throws the body in the air in order to experience the falling down or stamping on the floor with greater intensity.

This curious primary activity of man is, however, a preparation, or only the first stage of a most complicated system of activities. As such, it can be investigated, and the elements of action contained in it can be registered.

In studying a baby during the first few months of his life, we see that his movements are two-sided, both legs kicking simultaneously, the independent moving of one side of the body only being acquired or learnt later. The weight of the limbs is overcome by using a relatively great amount of muscular strength. The kicks are direct, leading in one direction only. The movements are relatively quick, and rhythmically repeated at fairly regular time intervals. Series of several kicks are used; isolated single kicks are very rare. Expressed in terms of effort study, the actions are thrusts or punches.

The arm actions are more flexible, but also strong and quick, and can be recognised as the actions of hitting out or slashing.

Flexible or indirect movement of the whole body, involving wringing and twists, at whatever speed, can be seen only as the result of discomfort, and in the face-muscles when the infant cries. Other signs of effort are present in his attempts to make sounds, which also are relatively strong and quick, except for the long-drawn-out wailing in discomfort.

This concentration on mainly strong, quick, and direct elements of action clearly shows the goal of development. The missing elements have to be acquired. This is promoted by external impressions. Although a baby does not imitate movements observed at this early age, he responds readily to stimuli, when he kicks, and later reaches towards a moving object. This, of course, only happens when the narrow world with which the baby was exclusively concerned has widened through the stirrings of his body and with this, recognition of his surroundings, at first somewhat blurred, has developed.

Grasping and gathering actions exerted upon the source of food—the mother's breast or the bottle—appear relatively early, and are still hasty and strong. A sustained reaching out for things arises only in that contemplative period in which the infant becomes more conscious of the surrounding wonder-world. All kinds of flexible and sustained stretchings are done when the first attempts at locomotion appear. It is at this period that the movements show a certain flow, which means that we can now discern at first some bound movements, and later fluent ones, revealing obvious control and regulation of effort combinations.

This control is, of course, far from being conscious in the adult sense of the word. Control is even without purpose in the sense of the accomplishment of a series of actions to the point where a certain desired effect is reached. Movements seeming to be aimless and ending abruptly for no apparent reason are very frequent. But there is no doubt that the movements of the child become increasingly controlled from a certain age onwards, until later they are to a fairly great extent consciously controlled, or at least controllable.

Another peculiarity of the child's movements must be mentioned. In the early stages of life all movements involve a large number of joints to such a degree that bodily stirrings are never confined to one joint alone. The total stir of the whole being is illustrated by the combination of kicking and making noises, which may have a parallel in the combination of song and dance in primitive folklore.

It is obvious that when only one joint is moved, a repression of the rest of the bodily stir takes place. This repression has an inhibitive character which is felt as a discomfort as long as the urge to move is as intensive as it is with any normal child. The natural outlet for this inner tension is dancing, and this is apparently one of the causes of the urge to dance awakening in children at an age when the controlled use of a restricted number of joints has become habitual.

When the child can stand and walk we see changes in his choice of movement. He still repeats rhythmic actions for the sake of moving and for no outwardly apparent reason. This is seen in continual jumping, connected sometimes with regular beating of the arms; the child enjoys the rhythm of the noise made, and here we have the spontaneous urge to dance. But dancing is a special kind of movement, and other more purposeful activities come into the forefront. The different activities of the child observed at this stage, such as the imitation of adult actions, the following of mental impulses to experience things, to feel or to know more about the wonders of his surroundings, always have the same common result—movement—and the same common source—effort.

Considering the lack of any real practical purpose or usefulness of these early activities, one can say that the only aim is the child's instinctive desire to develop his efforts. The growth of efforts in number, intensity, and refinement is the expression of the living energy within. *Effort* is the common denominator for the various strivings of the body and mind which become observable in the child's activity. Sporadic efforts are developed naturally through playing and are later refined through the discipline of dancing. Dance is an activity in which the spontaneous growth and blossoming of efforts are preserved up to adult age, and, indeed, when appropriately fostered, throughout the whole life.

Since in our civilisation this is all too rarely done, we can understand why in adolescents and adults of to-day the urge to dance decreases proportionally with the increase of their age. They are simply overwhelmed by their day-to-day duties and the manifold isolated efforts which their activities demand. The co-ordination of a greater number of joints becomes finally as impossible for the adult as was the use of isolated joints for the very small child.

It is, however, not only the collaboration of a number of joints, but that of the well-proportioned use of a number of different efforts, which makes dance movements pleasing and salutary. If we consider the very simple case of a child's rhythmic jumping, we shall easily recognise that such actions as pressing, thrusting, flicking, floating which may be compounded in the effort expression of the jump, must be finely balanced with each other, and that this balance must be kept throughout the whole series of repetitions.

We have stated that dancing relieves the feeling of discomfort produced by the repression of general bodily stirrings during isolated joint actions. We said that this is one of the causes of the urge to dance. There is another cause, no less imperious, namely, that the general bodily stir for which dance gives an outlet consists of a repeatedly performed series of simultaneous efforts which are finely balanced with each other, and this balance gives an aesthetic pleasure, like the colour-scheme in a picture or the harmony of sounds in music.

Children develop into individuals with definite characteristics, likes, and dislikes. When young they learn to imitate and, what is more important, to be influenced by adult ideas. In acquiring, and sometimes being forced to acquire, the adult's ideal of relative immobility, they lose the spontaneous drive to dance, which means the opportunity to balance their growing habit of using isolated efforts. They lose the taste for the enjoyment of the balance of effort qualities, and sometimes all traces of artistic taste which they had formerly shown may entirely disappear.

Parents and educationists who have felt this lack themselves, and who seek the causes of these frustrations, will do well to take into consideration the findings of modern dance research. They might then decide that dance tuition in schools and dancing in general is a valuable asset for the removal of these frustrations. If they do so, they will without doubt acknowledge that the study of the early behaviour of the children under their care can be a useful basis for the right form of dance training. The observation of the child undertaken for this purpose should, of course, not stop at these early stages.

The experience in which a child indulges, mainly in repetitive dance-like movements when he is restless or unoccupied, leads some people to the idea that a child must be kept employed with some useful-looking activity, in order to avoid the nonsensical excitement of rhythmic jumping. The result is that the child performs more and more isolated movements which are never balanced by what might be called an immersion into the flow of movement. Such an immersion is like a refreshing swim of twofold importance; it cleanses and it is enjoyable.

Dance tuition in schools has to provide the opportunity for this refreshing swim, which is at least as important as real swimming. As in the latter, the instructor will not just drop the child into the water, but will try to teach it a suitable technique, so the teacher of dance will seek a procedure by which the natural urge of the child is supplemented and its scope enlarged.

In working out the best way in which to begin dance training for young children, we can base the choice of movements on those which the baby uses instinctively when he begins to move. At first the child does not imitate, but reacts to stimuli, so the teacher should not ask children to copy at the beginning, but guide them through suggestion. They should be encouraged to use their own ideas and efforts, without being corrected to comply with adult standards of movement, which

are conditioned by convention, and therefore un-
natural. Correction and formal guidance come later,
when the child has developed his personality without
restrictions or inhibitions, and can understand and
appreciate the full significance of what is demanded.

At this early stage the use of repetition is valuable
and natural. Movements should involve the whole
body, or both arms or both legs together, and the
teacher should not demand precision or concentration
on one aspect of dance training, such as footwork, or
impose formations such as circles or lines, as the child
is not ready for these restrictions on his individuality.
The child should be given every opportunity to develop
his own expression through efforts of his own choosing.
Dance movements should be evolved from the strong,
direct, quick type of effort; light sustained movements
develop naturally later.

As the child grows older and more able to express
himself, one sees movements characteristic of the future
personality. The later stage in an infant's development
includes the urge to imitate, so that the teacher can
now give the child opportunities of watching others
and immediately performing what has been observed,
thus developing the sense of movement observation and
an increasing consciousness of action at the same time.

In the early stages there is always a danger of losing
the child's spontaneity by over-correction, and allowing
self-consciousness to creep in as the result of super-
imposing adult conceptions of movement.

It is valuable at this stage to develop the flow of the
child's actions using a sequence of movements, so that
they are continuous and longer, thus gradually paving
the way for the introduction of effort actions containing

the element of sustainment. On the whole, the choice of efforts is still naturally restricted to thrusting, dabbing, beating, but should now include pressing and pulling. The children can make up sequences of their own and gradually learn to appreciate the difference between strong and light tensions as well as between sudden and sustained movements.

They can use one part of the body at a time, but it is decidedly harmful to take too many movements of isolated parts of the body, as the child still needs to use his whole body as a means of expression, and not to be technically interested in one part only. It is the happy combination of mind and body developing alongside each other for which the teacher should work without inhibiting the one or over-developing the other.

The teacher can see the child dealing with the motion factors of Time, Weight, Space, and Flow. First the child is mostly concerned with speed, enjoying quick actions, and gradually learning to move in a more sustained manner. Then the child comes into contact with resistance to weight; at first his movements are strong, but later he develops the lighter shades of effort. The child is not yet aware of the ubiquity of space, since he uses mainly straight movements. The teacher can awaken the child to an understanding of the relation of movement to his surroundings. The child readily responds to suggestions to "touch the ceiling," to "run to this or that wall," or to "reach as far out as he can." The child should first learn to use space imaginatively, before making acquaintance with regular designs of floor patterns or set directional movements.

The child can learn to appreciate narrowness and width and all the various places around the body towards which he can move. Dance training from its earliest stages is principally concerned with teaching the child to live, move, and express himself in the media which govern his life, the most important of which is the child's own flow of movement. This develops slowly, and in many cases never at all. If a child has flow he is in perfect harmony with all the motion factors and is mentally and physically happily adjusted to life, but this is not the case if there is no development of his natural flow.

The junior school child needs a slightly different approach, according to his or her development. The rudiments of a more systematic dance training are to be taught here, in preparation for the more creative and complex forms of dancing which are valuable at a later age. The child learns through a recognition of basic elements of movement, using everyday words, and the training is carried out more and more by real dance exercises. The child is interested in practical things, such as movement observation, involving tests, as in repeating a movement exactly as someone else has performed it, or in building a sequence of movements. Various means, such as cardboard shapes of directional signs which are laid out on the floor and then transposed into bodily performance, can be used for this purpose.

At this stage the teacher should include the whole gamut of efforts, and make them increasingly complex as the child develops.

A slightly unbalanced effort make-up can frequently be remedied by the child himself if he has the necessary freedom, but the teacher can do a great deal to help him develop all his faculties harmoniously. Dance training is especially important as academic studies become more intense in order to balance increasing intellectual efforts with action efforts, so that the child develops as a whole, physically, mentally, and emotionally. Thorough effort training can be achieved only through dancing, as gymnastics, games, dramatics, and art are more concerned with the result of actions, and not with the action process itself.

Dance training with children of twelve and upwards becomes more concerned with the mental approach to movement. Here we are less able to describe the outward action since it is now the moods of effort which are more often involved. Different combinations of efforts create different moods in the dancer, which are analogous to the moods induced by combinations of colours in all their subtle varieties.

The child, as any adult, can have two attitudes to the various motion factors: either to fight against them—that is to activate a force of a transitive character which predominantly produces an objective function—or to give way to them—that is to enter a state of an intransitive character when predominently yielding to a subjective movement sensation. He can learn to appreciate the moods of sustained or sudden, firm or light, and flexible or direct movements. At twelve, the basic effort actions should be so much a habit that the finer shades of moods can now be more clearly realised.

Older children feel the need for finished dances and the feeling of working towards something definite, while the younger child's foremost need is for movement plays based on effort training.

CHAPTER III

SIXTEEN BASIC MOVEMENT-THEMES

In this century new forms of dancing have sprung up in the spheres of education and recreation, as well as in the theatre, which show a clear tendency to liberate the steps and gestures from the fetters of a too restricting style of movement.

Dance, which provides a counterbalance to the unceasing pursuit of practical aims, has, in common with everyday working actions, the use of bodily movements. In fact, it is influenced by the movement habits and demands prevailing at a particular period. Therefore, students of the contemporary forms of expressive movement must take into consideration all shapes and rhythms which correspond to the great variety of movements developed in our industrial civilisation.

While the movements of everyday life are directed towards the accomplishment of tasks connected with the practical needs of existence, in dance and play this practical aim recedes into the background. In the first case the mind directs the movement, in the other the movement stimulates activity of the mind.

Modern dance training has to be based on the knowledge of the stimulating power which movement exerts on the activities of the mind. The impact of movement on the mind has been studied, and it has been found that bodily movements consist of elements which create actions reflecting the particular qualities of the inner effort from which they spring. The spectator is highly sensitive to the combination of elements of movement without knowing why. It is the dancer's business to study the rules of co-ordination of the various effort qualities.

Dance as a composition of movement can be compared with spoken language. As words are built up of letters, so are movements built up of elements; as sentences are built up of words, so are dance phrases built up of movements. This language of movement, according to its content, stimulates activity of the mind in a similar but perhaps more complex manner than the spoken word.

In a free dance technique, that is a technique without a preconceived or dictated style, the whole range of the elements of movement is experienced and practised. From the spontaneous combination of these elements arises the almost unlimited variety of steps and gestures which is at the dancer's disposal.

Dance movements are basically the same as those used in everyday activities. The training should make the pupil able and agile to follow any voluntary or involuntary impulse to move with ease and security.

Where does the impulse of motion come from?—The impulse given to our nerves and muscles which move the joints of our limbs originates in inner efforts.

In training, the teacher has to stimulate the motion impulses of the student. He must study the systematic order of the different types of action resulting from the different qualities of the inner effort; thus effort control becomes possible.

Knowledge of both the co-ordination of efforts and the natural harmonies of the paths of movements in space, as well as experience of the interplay of the two, enables the teacher to create movement-themes, which can be used for recreative and educative purposes.

Where does the impulse of motion lead?—Into space. Therefore the mastery of movement in the surrounding space is necessary. One of the aims of training is, therefore, to enable the mover to reach every point of the spatial sphere surrounding the body. People can be made aware of those areas in space which are more easily reached by certain parts of the body than by others, according to its anatomic structure. This awareness must be acquired through practical movement experience. In this way one can learn to distinguish the main zones of the upper or lower limbs and those concerned with the right or the left side of the body.

Such zones are inter-connected by gestures creating pathways in space which not only have characteristic visible form but in their execution call for sensitive adjustment of bodily tension which arises from the relationship between the changing spatial inclinations of the path and the demands of balance. There is a logical order underlying the evolutions of the various shapes in space which can be realised in scales. Scales are graduated series of movements which pass through space in a particular order of balancing tensions according to a specified scheme of relations of the spatial inclinations. The student of movement has to become acquainted with the laws of harmony of movement in space.

Modern dance is based on the large range of everyday movements of contemporary man, and the best way of giving the teacher a methodical foundation on which to build the details of his tuition had to be developed through many years. Instead of sets of standardised exercises, basic themes of movement and their combinations and variations have proved to be the most helpful tool for the teacher of the contemporary form of dance.

The leading idea is that the teacher should find his own manner of stimulating his pupils to move, and later to dance, by choosing from a collection of basic movement-themes those variations which are appropriate to the actual stage and state of development of a pupil or of the majority of a class. The collection is built up along a scale of increasing complexity corresponding roughly to the development of a child from the infant stage to the highest age-group.

Each of the basic movement-themes represents a movement idea corresponding to a stage in the progressive unfolding of the feel of movement in the growing child, and in later stages to the development of his mental understanding of the principles involved.

Each basic movement-theme contains many possible variations. Some themes or their variations can be combined with each other; others may be joined with one another through transmutations of their details. The movement ideas contained in one theme need not be fully assimilated by the pupil before another theme is started. Movement ideas can develop parallel to each other, and some teachers might find in relatively advanced themes details which they may use as an incentive in comparatively early stages of dance tuition. On the other hand, the most elementary movement themes will remain valuable even for the highest age-groups. They can be usefully applied in any of the later stages. Adults perform early play forms with as much pleasure as small children when the themes are presented in the right spirit and at the right moment.

The sixteen basic movement-themes described in this chapter can be divided into elementary themes (1 to 8) appropriate for children under eleven years of age, and advanced themes (9 to 16) corresponding to the needs of children over eleven years of age.

Practical examples from the history of dance and information gained through movement research, which show the association of dance movement with various occupations of man, may convey to adolescents an appreciation of dance as an important factor of our life.

The basic themes of movement and their variations can serve as material for the building up of movement studies and dances of educational value.

The average dance teacher will content himself with building up longer coherent movement studies without having an ambition to become a composer of dances, which is an artistic profession of its own. Children should invent their dances freely as a creative activity very similar to that fostered in modern art education.

ELEMENTARY MOVEMENT-THEMES

1. Themes concerned with the awareness of the body

A baby plays with his arms, legs, fingers, and toes. The growing child can be made aware of the possibility of playfully using shoulders, elbows, wrists, fingers, hips, knees, heels, toes, head, chest, back, or any other areas of the body for moving and dancing.

2. Themes concerned with the awareness of weight and time

The growing child can be made aware that the movements of any part of the body (see Theme 1) can be either sustained or sudden as well as strong or light.

3. Themes concerned with the awareness of space

The growing child can be made aware of the difference between narrow and wide movements. Apart from the extension of any part of the body into space or its approach to the centre of the body, the awareness of the room in which the body moves, with its floor, walls, and ceiling, is a useful theme for the development of the sense of space and its fundamental directions.

4. Themes concerned with the awareness of the flow of the weight of the body in space and time

The continuity of movement in straight lines as well as in roundabout and twisted pathways with different speeds and in various rhythms, which can be clapped or sung or beaten on drums, leads from playing to play forms.

The plasticity of the body, that is its sculptural form, can be felt in different positions in which the flow of movement is stopped. A simple catchword for small children is "Make a statue."

5. Themes concerned with the adaptation to partners

The solitary "statue" can change its position in response to another "statue" represented by a partner.

Stimulation can be given through showing the difference between large, tall, wide-reaching statues and those of narrow, small, huddled positions.

Later the positions can be extended to short response sequences. One partner moves and the other responds, and so on.

Contrast in speed—quick against slow—and in direction—straight against roundabout—can be added.

The repetition of short responses trains the memory of movement as a feeling in the body.

When the changing movements of a leader are followed by a group, the movement imagination of the leader and the capacity of observation and quick response of the members of the group can be awakened. The feeling of belonging together in a group is strengthened.

6. Themes concerned with the instrumental use of the limbs of the body

The hands can be used as instruments, as pincers in gripping, or as spoons for scooping, and the legs are used mainly for locomotion—that is, they are instruments to move the body from one place to another. The normal functions of the limbs, such as gripping, scooping, and scattering movements of hands and arms and stepping, running, leaping, and turning movements produced by the feet and legs, can alternate with gathering, shovelling, and strewing gestures of legs while balancing on different parts of the body and with crawling, somersaulting, running on all fours, and so on, in which hands and arms are partly used for locomotion.

7. Themes concerned with the awareness of isolated actions

Basic effort actions, such as pressing, thrusting, or flicking performed by various parts of the body, can later be performed into various directions of space. Each action has a typical speed. The repetition of isolated actions will thus prove to be a means of developing the ability to produce, on the one hand, a series of sudden discharges of movement impulses following one another quickly, and on the other, a series of prolonged discharges which are undertaken in slow succession.

The feeling for accents in rhythm is awakened through repetitions of strong movements. Light efforts bring the awareness of fine touch movements without losing tension entirely.

8. Themes concerned with occupational rhythms

Primitive working actions awaken the feeling of transitions between efforts. For example, in sawing, chopping, pulling a rope, hammering, screwing, ironing, scything, digging or stitching, sewing, cutting different materials, whisking, chopping *et cetera*, the main action is followed by a relaxation before being repeated. Such a relaxation is not simply a fading away of energy; it contains a set of elements of movement which momentarily help to dissolve those of the main action, thus preparing for its effective repetition. Awareness of the rhythm of exertion and recovery is strengthened by a series of separate or different working actions which are interspersed with appropriate transitional qualities.

Although these actions are led by arms and hands, the participation of the whole body, and especially the change of stance—that means, the transference of the weight of the body producing steps, is to be taken carefully into consideration.

Note on the elementary themes 1-8

The first eight basic movement-themes are appropriate for children of Primary age.

The themes are interconnected because in all of them all parts of the body and all the contrasts of Weight, Space, and Time can be used.

Dance plays with a story should be used sparingly. The experience of movement imagination and memory of movement is a stimulus strong enough to make longer combinations of themes into movement studies interesting and enjoyable for the children.

Towards the end of the junior age-group simple forms of the advanced themes (9-16) can be worked into the elementary themes (1-8). The latter should, however, remain the fundament of all dance teaching in the lower age-groups.

ADVANCED MOVEMENT-THEMES

9. Themes concerned with the shapes of movement

The drawing or writing of small and large patterns in the air can be best stimulated by writing numbers or letters (e.g. initials of Christian names) into all directions of the sphere of movement.*

The progressive increase in the size of the pattern should finally fill the greatest possible extension of the sphere of movement, the patterns being performed as fluently as possible. Turning round while writing in the air can be used in order to increase flow and flexibility.

The difference between angular and curved patterns should be experienced; for example, the difference

* See Chap. V, p. 85.

between a triangle and a circle of the same size and
made in the same position.

10. Themes concerned with combinations of the eight basic effort actions

Themes containing transitions between two or
several basic effort actions can be elicited from
sequences, such as:

(*a*) Wring, Press, Glide, Float, Flick.
(*b*) Wring, Float, Flick, Slash, Punch.
(*c*) Wring, Slash, Flick, Dab, Glide.

The eight basic efforts are: Wring, Press, Glide,
Float, Flick, Slash, Punch, Dab. Each of these efforts
contains three of the six movement elements: firm,
light, sustained, sudden, direct, flexible.*

It will be seen that each of the efforts in the above
sequences is transmuted into the next by changing one
effort element only. The effort actions in these sequences
are primarily akin to one another.

Many such sequences of two, three, or more basic
effort actions can be found.

Later on, sequences of efforts being secondarily akin
—that means containing a change of two elements—can
be used.

Contrasting efforts in which all three elements are
changed are most difficult, indeed, almost impossible
to perform in immediate sequence without strong concentration.

The whole series of the eight basic effort actions can
be performed in a coherent sequence in which couples
of contrasting and akin efforts might alternate.

* See R. Laban and F. C. Lawrence, *Effort*, and R. Laban
Mastery of Movement.

An example of such a sequence with an alternation of contrasting and secondarily akin effort couples is:

Float contrasts Punch which is secondarily akin to Glide
Glide   ,,   Slash   ,,   ,,   ,,   Dab
Dab   ,,   Wring   ,,   ,,   ,,   Flick
Flick   ,,   Press   ,,   ,,   ,,   Float
et cetera.

The performance of the series can be repeated without interruption between the repetitions.

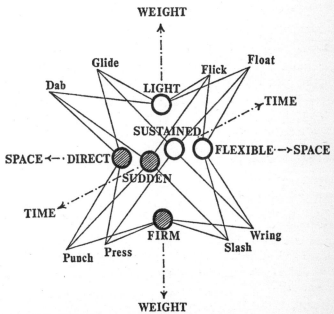

FIG. 1.—The six effort elements and the eight basic effort actions. Shaded circles show elements fighting against, open circles show elements indulging in, weight or space or time (see also Chapter IV).

Each sequence of basic effort actions has its own rhythm according to the Time elements contained in the efforts constituting the sequence.

11. Themes concerned with space orientation

Sequences of movements can be performed so that each movement is directed to a certain point in the space round the body and the change from one point to the next is harmonious and flowing, forming definite patterns; that means with a definite space orientation. See Fig. 2.

These patterns may extend chiefly in the air around the body, when they are known as peripheral, or they may pass close to the centre of the body, and are called central. Patterns most frequently combine both central and peripheral movements.*

It will be seen that some patterns have a characteristic form which can be introduced to younger age-groups as shapes which are familiar to them.

For example, it has been found useful to call the pattern: *dl—hl—hr—dr—dl* the "door" as an aid for memory. (The meaning of the abbreviations *dl—hl—hr et cetera* is explained in Fig. 2, p. 37.)

In the same way one might call the pattern:

lb—lf—rf—rb—lb the "table,"

or the pattern:

db—hb—hf—df—db the "wheel."

* At a stage of development where the writing in the air of numbers and letters is practical as a theme for shape awareness, it is advantageous to ease the transition from the free shapes to the themes of space orientation by giving the regular shapes a name instead of burdening the child's mind with names of points and directions.

Many patterns will show zigzag form, or, when the corners are rounded, circle, spiral, and other familiar forms.

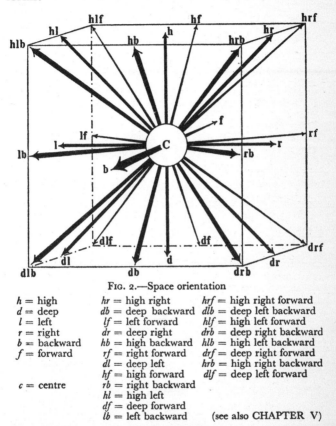

FIG. 2.—Space orientation

h = high	hr = high right	hrf = high right forward
d = deep	db = deep backward	dlb = deep left backward
l = left	lf = left forward	hlf = high left forward
r = right	dr = deep right	drb = deep right backward
b = backward	hb = high backward	hlb = high left backward
f = forward	rf = right forward	drf = deep right forward
	dl = deep left	hrb = high right backward
	hf = high forward	dlf = deep left forward
c = centre	rb = right backward	
	hl = high left	
	df = deep forward	
	lb = left backward	(see also CHAPTER V)

The performance of any kind of shapes or patterns must become so automatised that they are conceived in the mind and felt in the body as a whole phrase of movement and not as a composite of lines. A valuable means of achieving this is the rounding of the corners so that the movement does not stop at the points of orientation. In other cases, and especially in the beginning of the use of orientation themes, such stops are instructive. It is useful to introduce changes of front—turns of all kinds, somersaults, *et cetera*, when following directions leading backwards. But directions and shapes lying behind the back should also be performed without changing the front. The flexibility of the spine is increased through the bendings and twistings needed for such movements.*

Accelerations of speed during the performance of one definite shape can be usefully introduced at later stages. So also can slowing down.

All shapes and regular patterns can be performed in two ways, that means the order of their points can be reversed, in starting at the end point and retracing the path to the point of departure.

12. Themes concerned with shapes and efforts using different parts of the body

Any shape or regular pattern can be performed in conjunction with any effort or can contain any sequence

---

* The themes of space orientation can be performed, like the free shapes (Theme 9), in small, medium, and large extension. The moving person can stop at any point on the way from the centre to the most distant point which he can reach. There exist, for example, many points *hf*, distributed along the line *c* to *hf*. The distinction of a narrow *hf* (level with shoulders), a medium distance *hf* (level with forehead), and a wide *hf* (reaching as far as possible), will suffice for training purposes.

The rhythm of the movements along orientation patterns can be chosen as one wishes, but it is advisable to start with regular time intervals, each stretch in space having the same time duration.

of efforts. Certain shapes or patterns will, however, combine better with certain efforts or effort sequences than with others.

Any shape or regular pattern can contain one or more efforts. For instance, the pattern *dl—hl—hr—dr* (or its reversion *dr—hr—hl—dl*) * can be performed with a continuous pressing movement or with any other effort. But it can also be performed on some of the stretches of the shape with pressing and on other stretches with another effort.

It is difficult to perform some movements in directions in which parts of the body are not habitually extended, say, pressing with the foot high forward or with palms behind the back.

Effort actions are more naturally performed in certain regions around the body than in others. Everybody will turn towards an object upon which he desires to exert a pressure with the hand; in this sense, the region of the sphere of movement into which a pressure is most easily exerted is *f*, and all its combinations *rf*, *hf*, *lf*, *df*, *et cetera*. It will be noticed, however, that pressing with the palm of the right hand in the direction of *lf* is easier than in the direction of *rf*, and the converse when the left palm is used. A pressure towards *df* is easier with either arm than towards *hf*. Instead of the arm, any other part of the body—say, shoulder, elbow, hip, or knee—can be used, and their pressure exerted in different directions will show various degrees of ease.

The easy performance of certain efforts in definite directions or along stretches of free shapes or regular patterns makes the movement harmonious. The body is brought by grotesque movements into contorted

* See points around the body, Fig. 2, p. 37.

positions when reaching in an awkwardly situated direction with an unsuitable effort. Other efforts in the same relatively awkward direction exerted by the same part of the body might be less disharmonious.

The experience of less easy combinations of directions, shapes, and efforts should not be excluded from the dance curriculum as has been done in many of the traditional dance forms in which gracefulness and prettiness of the body carriage was the main ideal.

It is possible to describe shapes or regular patterns with any part of the body; one can draw a whole pattern with a shoulder, with an elbow or a knee, *et cetera*, or the first part of a pattern could be shaped with the elbow, after which the shoulder would take over the lead, and a third portion of the pattern might be drawn by the hand, starting with the finger-tips.

The combinations are almost unlimited; as we have seen limbs other than the starting limb can take over the lead at some stage of the pattern, and it is thus quite possible that after the finger-tips have had the lead, one of the knees will continue the pattern and a step may follow.

In everyday life we can observe the linking together of almost any part of the body with any other in performing the patterns prescribed by our work. This linking can happen not only consecutively but also simultaneously. More than one part of the body may at the same time participate in creating the shape and effort expression of the movement.

In standing on one leg the other leg and the two arms, head and trunk are free to change their position in a variety of ways. The variations depend on which shapes, efforts and body parts combine or follow one another in the action.

13. Themes concerned with elevation from the ground

Of all body activities the skips, leaps, and jumps are considered the most characteristic dancing actions, because they often constitute the main content of a whole dance.

The suspension of the body in the air is followed by a fall on to one or both legs. The transitory stance helps to gain the elastic impulse needed for the next leap through the air. In everyday life we may jump over an obstacle, but this remains an isolated action. In dance, however, the state of suspense can be continuously repeated as the main theme.

While in ordinary walking steps only one leg tends towards a definite direction in space, while the other leg is bound with the foot to the ground, in the themes of elevation from the ground both legs and feet tend either together towards one, or separately towards two, directions. The basic idea of this movement theme is, therefore, concerned with the directional movement of the legs combined with corresponding efforts in the lower parts of the body. The directions of the legs will rarely be other than—*d*, *dl*, *dr*, *db*, *df*, *f*, *b*, *l*, *r*, *lf*, *rf*, *lb*, *rb*. The high directions might be attempted or approached exceptionally in acrobatic jumps and kicks.

The efforts felt in the legs are strong and elastically thrusting at the moment before leaving the ground, but a wide range of hits, slashings, floatings, dabs, and indeed any other imaginable effort, can be used.

The upper part of the body is either relatively effortless, without following other directions than those of the jump, or performs shapes or patterns of its own. It is, indeed, possible to perform any of the above-mentioned movements with all their combinations of shapes and efforts while flying through the air, though more complicated movements will necessarily have to be relatively small in extension and of short duration. Turning leaps of all kinds increase the fluency of the movement.

The contrast between movements performed in kneeling, sitting, lying on the floor, and flying movements in the air stresses the intensity of elevation.

14. Themes concerned with the awakening of group feeling

Crowds of dancers without definite group formations can move like one body. In the beginning this will be most strongly felt in common rising and sinking, or in the performance of common precipitation, whirling around a group centre, and similar evolutions.

The contrast consists of individual movements made in a crowd. The same effort can be made by the individuals, but each one moving into directions of his own choice. Different efforts of everybody's own choice made into various directions or along shapes of their own choice lead to groupings which should be kept for a short time in a definite position. The exact repetition of such group improvisations enriches imagination and strengthens the memory of movement.

The observation of one group by another is useful for the development of the feel for plasticity of group movement and the conscious discernment of group co-ordination.

One group of dancers can respond to the movements of another group. The repetition of such counter-moves, while keeping the exact space proportions and distances between the individuals, furthers the sensitive adaptation to the movements of others. This is an excellent preparation for the performance of dances with group feeling.

15. Themes concerned with group formations

The simplest group formations—row and circle—can wax and wane. A row can be stretched or shortened, whereby the distances between the individuals increase or decrease. At first the individuals should all perform the same movements, except the steps which might differ in extension and number when leading to the waxing and waning of a formation.

A row can shrink towards one of its ends or towards a centre within the row. In the same way it can grow from one of the ends to the other or from a centre to both ends.

The shrinking and growing of a circle can be done around the centre of a circle or towards a point within the circle.

The movements and rhythms by which the waxing and waning is produced or accompanied are almost endless in their variety.

A row can run straight or in a curve or turn into a circle, just as the circle can open into a row.

Angular floor patterns can be introduced as a variation. Any formation desired can result from an exact set of steps and movements performed with various efforts.

Groups can move on different levels, some sitting, some kneeling, some standing. Groupings can be symmetric or asymmetric.

Crowd work and formation work can alternate with each other in more complex movement studies and dances.

16. Themes concerned with the expressive qualities or moods of movements

Just as the letters of the alphabet are compounded into words, and the words arranged into sentences, so are the simple elements of motion compounded into more complex movements, and finally into phrases of dance.

The significance of the compounds of movements is not conventional as is that of the words and sequences of language. The sense of the phrases of movement can, however, be understood as the expression of definite action moods. It must be made clear what dance or movement can really express.

In modern dance research this problem has been thoroughly investigated, and it has been found that it is erroneous to take dance as the language of the emotion only. It is rather a language of action in which the various intentions and bodily and mental efforts of man are arranged into coherent order.

We can recognise in dancing an organised co-opera-tion of our mental, emotional, and bodily powers resulting in actions the experience of which is of the greatest importance to the development of the child's personality. The child exercises the co-operation of these powers from birth onwards, first unconsciously and later to a certain extent consciously. Dancing can be understood as an attempt to assimilate the rules of the fluent co-ordination of the operation of body and mind through the practical experience of the many combinations of its constituents.

In producing a definite action the dancer is not always conscious of the combination of efforts from which the mood results. The feeling of simple action moods is strengthened by the repetition of a simple effort. More complicated action moods result from combined sequences or from different efforts. The repetition of each sequence strengthens the feeling for the mood it contains.

The order in the manifoldness of movements and the assimilation of that order as a whole, is enjoyable, but it is characterised, too, by varying degrees of clearness and perfection.

Dance movements are best explained as combinations of the elements of movement resulting in action moods. The translation into words is possible when the result of an effort is recognised as an action, say, of dramatic content. In other cases the translation into words is less easy, because we lack terms to describe the complex shapes and rhythms of movement resulting from the consecutive performance of several efforts. In these cases the translation into words would be too cumbersome and is better replaced by special technical terms.

The moods or expressions of movements have a double source. It will be easily understood that a body and arm stretched high and wide has a different expression from that of a body huddled up on the floor. It would be wrong, however, to speak of definite moods expressed by positions, because the dancer can move into any position in very different ways. Suppose he reaches the highly stretched position on one occasion with a soft floating movement and another time with an energetic thrust. It is obvious that the mood of the movement will be different each time. The expression of a movement depends therefore on several factors—space location, including shape, and dynamic content, including effort.

Everybody will be able to imagine and to feel the mood of a sustained movement as contrasted with the mood expressed in a sudden movement. What he might not consider at first is the additional shade which the direction or shape of the movement gives to its mood.

Clear contrasts of mood are felt in the effort elements:

> either firm   or light
> ,,   direct ,, flexible
> ,,   sudden ,, sustained
> ,,   bound ,, free

Applying this classification to basic effort actions, one will understand that, say, "gliding" incorporates the moods of sustainment, lightness, and directness, or "thrusting" the moods of swiftness, strength, and directness, and so on.

The moods, however, do not accumulate only in effort compounds, as, for instance, in the basic effort actions. Following one another in movement sequences, the consecutive efforts will build up a kind of melody or sentence-like sequence, the collective mood of which is an important part of movement experience.

It seems that the moods are strongly influenced by the difference of the mixtures of effort elements, in which the fighting or indulging attitudes towards Weight, Space, or Time are balanced in a greater or lesser degree.

The mood of floating, in which all elements derive

from an "indulging" attitude, will fundamentally differ
from the mood of thrusting, in which all elements derive
from an attitude of "fighting."

On the other hand, the mood of dabbing will, in spite
of its lightness, differ essentially from a floating mood,
because dabbing contains two "fighting" elements and
one element only resulting from an "indulging"
attitude.

Although this may sound complicated, it is a very
simple fact which is, of course, less easy to explain in
such clear words or names as those attributed from time
immemorial, say, to the mixtures of colours. Only very
few mixtures of efforts have names—only the basic
effort actions and their moods are fairly obvious to
everybody.

The moods of movement need to be considered when
one wants to understand more fully the experience of
the dancer who plays with effort rhythms, and the
impression of the spectator who enjoys the effort
rhythms seen in dancing. The dance teacher must know
about the moods of movement, because the new dance
technique is built up on mutations or changes of efforts
appearing in the flow of movement, which are the
bearers of the moods of movement.

The shape of a movement and the part of the body
which performs it do not change the fundamental mood
contained in the effort, but the spatial location of the
movement may give the mood an additional shade.

Moods of movement are involved in the characterisa-
tion of types which the actor represents on the stage.
These characters have been seen in life, using certain
shapes and rhythms of movement, frequently with a
typical body location of the effort. Looking at such

types mainly from the point of view of effort, one will notice that, say, a person who continuously uses dabbing movements as the accompaniment of his speech will differ greatly from a person who habitually uses wringing movements. A discussion in efforts, where two persons are dancing together—the one, say, mainly using dabbing, and the other wringing—will give an amusing introduction to the use of moods of movement.

Any discussion between two persons mainly using two different basic efforts will give the opportunity of discerning new shades of the moods of movement. Movement studies of this kind approach dramatic expression, but they also help to clarify an important sector of dance study. No matter whether the theme of the discussion is a quarrel, a loving approach, or an indifferent social chat, the contrast between the characters, each with his different effort make-up, remains the same. The shades added to the mood by different shapes, rhythms, and body locations of the movements are related to the story and the emotions felt during the various happenings.

Themes concerned with the expressive qualities of the moods of movement cover an enormous field and can give scope to almost limitless variations. Studying such themes gives an insight into the connection between the structure of movement sequences and the personal characteristics of an individual.

The important fact for the dance teacher, however, is that children of the later senior age-group have an urge to explore their own and other people's moods. Much help can be given to them when dance tuition in these critical years is adapted to the aim of clearing up the sources of irritating situations and habits and making them thus less important and less dangerous.

Note on the advanced themes 9-16

Exercises or dance sequences calling upon the body, the feeling, and the understanding of moods, should all be included throughout the whole period of methodical dance tuition, from the junior age up to school-leaving age. But the stress laid on one or the other of these typical forms of dancing should vary according to the development and momentary needs of the majority of the pupils in a class.

The final success of a well developed and well ordered effort-life, towards which the baby already starts to strive, can be achieved, and the pupil leaving school can have acquired that poise of personality which today is often lacking because of the lop-sided development of the intellectual faculty, contrasted only with a rough-and-ready impetuosity of movement or with exaggerated self-consciousness and rigidity.

The advanced themes are appropriate for the age-groups from later juniors on to school-leaving age. It will be obvious that for all these themes simpler variations can be found, which are appropriate to younger age-groups, while the more complicated variations will have to be reserved for higher age-groups. But, as has been mentioned several times, no exact limits can be drawn.

The development of variations and their application at the right place and at the right moment is one of the fundamental tasks of the dance teacher.

The dance plays of the higher age-groups will approach more and more what we are accustomed to consider as dance compositions. It should be mentioned here that the various forms of dance composition extending from the movement drama to the more lyrical group dances are manifold, because:

(*a*) The movement idea incorporated in the composition can be either complex or simple.

(*b*) The technical details of movements, shapes, and efforts used in a composition can be either complicated or simple.

The movement drama can be a story of tragic or comic content, but the conflict and solution of movement contrast are in themselves a dramatic affair, needing no excuse in a story, which might be built up around them.

In the same way, lyricism in dance is not a description of events in nature or of feeling, but a performance of movement sequences in which dramatically conflicting contrasts and their solution recede into the background.

It is very doubtful whether the average dance teacher will be able to compose elaborate dances without having studied the language of movement thoroughly. Moreover, it is desirable that children of higher age-groups should themselves invent their own dances.

Dance taken as a part of art education in school cannot ignore the creative activity of the pupil in this fundamental art. Therefore it may perhaps be helpful to say a little more about the dances of the higher age-groups of children and adolescents. Such themes have only been lightly touched upon in all the advanced movement-themes. However, the content of several themes or of some of their variations constitutes a sound basis for more elaborate dances.

Dynamic plays in which the precipitation and the withholding of individual or group movements are combined differ from formation plays, in which the eddies and waves of movement or rectilinear forms of individual and group movement prevail.

The rhythmic repetition of movement ideas contained in the themes is the simplest form of dance composition, which can consist of either predominantly dynamic or formative elements. The variations of a theme can be linked up into dances, and so can mutations into different kinds of themes.

For all this, neither dramatic nor musical inspiration from a text or set music is required. The accompaniment of the selected movement sequences can be supplied by wordless singing or percussion, both executed by a special group of the children, and sometimes by the dancing children themselves. The result will not be striking works of art or exemplary productions, but whatever is danced should be executed with full inner participation and clearness of form. The creative stimulus and the awareness of the enlivening and freeing influence of dance movement are all that is desirable.

The cultivation of artistic taste and discrimination in general cannot be furthered better or more simply than by the art of movement. Yet the dances which are produced must never originate from the wish to create outstanding works of art. Should such a miracle occur once, everybody will be pleased, but in schools we should not attempt to produce external success through effective performances.

CHAPTER IV

RUDIMENTS OF A FREE DANCE TECHNIQUE

VALUE OF EFFORT EXPERIMENTS

THE purpose of the following series of effort experiments is to introduce the teacher to the bodily sensation of movement as practised in modern educational dance. The systematic development of the teacher's effort capacity is something quite different from his method of teaching children. In our opinion the latter will best consist of a free adaptation of the above mentioned basic movement themes to the progressing needs of his classes. The collection of experiments in this chapter will mainly serve the teacher's personal movement experience, which, of course, involves the bodily performance of them connected with the mental assimilation of the underlying rules of effort coordination.

These experiments cannot attempt to cover the whole of the new dance technique, nor can they be anything more than a guide and stimulus to those who are interested. The essence of this contemporary form of dance movement is that each individual has scope in which to develop his own approach and to use his own interpretation.

The study of basic effort actions is fundamental for both the teacher and student for the development of a harmonious and balanced use of these actions in everyday life as well as in the art of dancing. It is easily observable that many people tend to over-emphasise certain actions which affects the ease and mastery of their movement. Other actions are neglected or used so sparingly that the natural range of effort expression becomes restricted.

Such disturbed effort balance, having a detrimental effect on individual and collective well-being and efficiency, is much more universal than is generally supposed. It can be remedied only by a person who has experienced the full range of human effort capacity and has a sufficient knowledge of the natural co-ordination of the different efforts with one another.

The basic effort actions are also present in any mental or intellectual form of expression, and the outward projection of an effort can be indicative of a state of mind. Some people may never have experienced either bodily or mentally some of the efforts described here, and it will be beneficial for them to enlarge their understanding and the appreciation of a wider range of movements together with the feeling and comprehension of human action which such movements stimulate.

Effort, relaxation, rest

The study of human actions and of the efforts underlying them is derived from investigations into the relationship between effort and relaxation, and of the rôle which these two important aspects of activity play in efficiency, economy of energy, and in the flow of movement.

Relaxation is often associated only with rest; that means, with the cessation of movement, say after exhaustion. Modern dance from its early days has emphasised the importance of swinging movement, in which a relatively relaxed phase of movement is compounded with a relatively stressed phase. An effort to attain lightness and buoyancy is made in a rhythmical interchange with an effort of weighty strength. It was, however, soon discovered that the time rhythm of a movement and the shape of its path through space are as important for the right proportion between exertion and relaxation as that between the changing degrees of its strength.

As soon as it was realised that relaxation can be active and can consist of movement it became obvious that it involves, as does any other movement, effort. The antithesis between effort and relaxation has thus lost its proper meaning.

Rest might be considered as relatively effortless, but not so relaxation. The finer shades of effort, once recognised, show certain co-ordinations which become visible in their external projection in movement. These co-ordinations are essential in free dance technique. They can be experienced experimentally when voluntarily produced and consciously felt.

The conscious distinction between the shades of efforts and actions can be enhanced by recording them with the help of appropriate graphs. The symbols used for the graphical representation of basic effort actions in industrial notation can be added to the description of effort experiments.*

* Readers interested in the principles on which the graphs are based are referred to *Effort*, by R. Laban and F. C. Lawrence, published by Macdonald & Evans. Further detailed references can be found in R. Laban's book *The Mastery of Movement*.

Movements and effort actions

Four main types of movement are easily discerned:

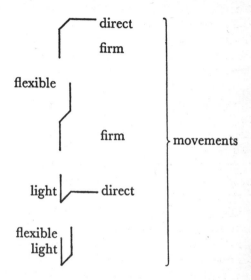

Each of these movements can have two character-istic time values: *sustained* or *sudden*.

Sustainment is recorded by a short line in the lower left corner of the graph, while suddenness is shown by a short line in the lower right corner.

The sign for effort, a short slanting stroke ╱, stands in the centre of the graph.

The signs for time values:

         ╱   ╱

       ——   ——

    sustained   sudden

added to the four signs of the main movements constitute the graphs of the eight basic effort actions:

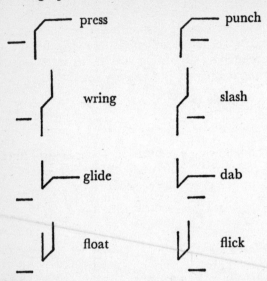

The best way of "getting the feel" of the basic effort actions is to perform all the variations of these actions as described in the following series of effort experiments, but mention shall first be made of the two characteristic flow values.

The experience of the flow of movement

In an action capable of being stopped and held without difficulty at any moment during the movement, the flow is *bound*.

In an action in which it is difficult to stop the movement suddenly, the flow is *free* or *fluent*.

As a sudden action reveals the underlying effort "to

be quick," so a bound or a fluent action reveals the underlying effort "to be bound or fluent."

The control of an action which results in free flow is recorded by means of a short line preceding the slanting effort stroke, and that which results in bound flow is represented by a short line succeeding it. Both meet the slanting effort stroke at its lower end, thus:

free _____/   ∠___ bound

The following combinations composed of fluency or boundness on the one hand, and sustainment or sudden-ness, on the other, are possible:

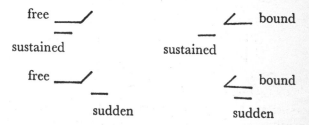

free _____/   ∠___ bound
  —   —
sustained   sustained

free _____/   ∠___ bound
      —   —
      sudden   sudden

It will be noticed that the first six actions described below have a different fluency:

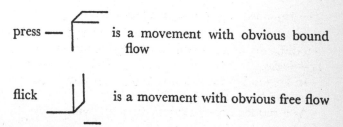

press ——⌐   is a movement with obvious bound
                    flow

flick ⎊   is a movement with obvious free flow

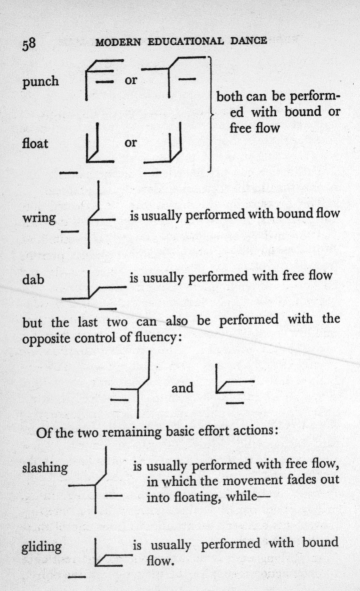

punch   or

float   or

} both can be perform-
ed with bound or
free flow

wring   is usually performed with bound flow

dab   is usually performed with free flow

but the last two can also be performed with the opposite control of fluency:

and

Of the two remaining basic effort actions:

slashing   is usually performed with free flow, in which the movement fades out into floating, while—

gliding   is usually performed with bound flow.

EIGHT BASIC EFFORT ACTIONS

1. Pressing

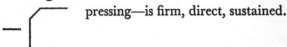 pressing—is firm, direct, sustained.

This action can best be felt first in the palms of the hands, then in the arms, shoulders, trunk, and legs.

The pressure in the hands can be directed into various zones, the most important being across the body and forward deep; but there are endless possibilities, with each hand separately, or both together, pressing downwards, upwards, across, sideways, forwards, and backwards, extending into space in all directions.

Pressing should also be experienced in other parts of the body, such as the shoulders, chest, back, hips, knees, and feet, extending not only into space away from the body, but also towards it. Other possible variations are pressing simultaneously with palms, or with different parts of the body into various directions, for example, hips move downwards, while the arms go forwards, *et cetera*.

Legs can exert pressure on to the floor while carrying or shifting the weight of the body or they can press up into the air into many different directions. These pressing actions can be combined with those of the palms, arms, or any other upper parts of the body. Pressing can be performed in standing, kneeling, sitting, or lying positions, as well as during walking. Pressing movements can serve as transitions from one of these positions to another.

In pushing away something concrete the resistance to one's action is supplied by the weight of the object, but if the object is now removed and the same feeling of pressure is produced, another set of muscles is called into play to provide the resistance. If these other muscles did not co-operate in providing resistance, one would fall forward in the attempt to push away a non-existent object. These antagonistic muscle groups, as they are called, work to produce a strong tension all over the body, so that even when pressing principally with the palms of the hands there is a counter-tension in the legs, trunk, and neck, giving a feeling of controlled strength.

"Fighting against" Weight and Space (i.e. producing strong resistance and following a one-directional pull) combined with "indulging in" Time (i.e. sustaining the action over a period of time), which is the essence of pressing, develops a valuable effort control. The steady, undeviating continuity of the counter-tension produces a special kind of controlled strength which is different from that met with in any other physical action.

A movement can be considered as strong and firm when the prevailing effort is of muscular tension, as opposed to muscular relaxation. Strong actions other than pressing are pushing, wringing, pulling, punching, thrusting, slashing, hitting (hard), throwing, *et cetera*.

Physically, strength or force is exerted by the pressure of weight, steam, the impact of a heavy object falling, rolling, and so on. This can be counteracted to a certain degree by strong bodily actions.

2. Flicking   flicking—is light, flexible, sudden.

This action should first be experienced in the hands with light, quick twists of the wrist and fingers, as if flicking away dust on one's clothes, and then repeated all round the body, high, low, far away, close in, and so on.

Flicking movements can be made with shoulders, head, and feet.

The most important zone in which flicking hands should be exercised lies on the open side and backwards high. But there are endless possibilities, e.g. flicking with each hand separately, or both together, downwards, upwards, across, sideways, forwards, and backwards, in fact into all directions of space.

Flicking should also be experienced in other parts of the body, such as the shoulders, elbows, hips, knees, and feet, not only moving into space away from the body, but also towards it. Other possible variations are flicking simultaneously with both hands but each into different directions, or flicking with different parts of the body into various directions—for example, one knee flicking sideways outwards, while the elbow of the other side of the body flicks backwards diagonally high, and so on.

A foot can be flicked into the air in many directions, or the flicking foot can touch the floor. Both feet can be flicked in the air in jumping. Flicking steps can be made as in tap dancing.

Flicking can be performed in standing, kneeling, sitting, or lying positions, and can be used as a transition from one position to the next.

In flicking away something concrete, or in flicking feet on to the floor, resistance to one's action is supplied by the surface of the object. In performing flicking in the air another set of muscles is called into play which causes a slight elastic rebound of the flicking limb.

Flicking done repeatedly produces a fluttering movement in which the recurrence of the rebound between the flicking actions establishes continuity of movement. The whole body can participate in flicking actions in which the feeling of intensive lightness and relaxed buoyancy is experienced.

"Indulging in" Weight (i.e. easing muscular tension and producing a feeling of lightness) and in Space (i.e. giving up a one-directional pull and yielding to the sensation of ubiquitousness) combined with "fighting against" Time (i.e. quickening the action so that it happens in a brief moment of time) is the essence of flicking. This combination develops a valuable effort control and gives an entirely different movement experience from that gained by simple relaxing shaking exercises. The elasticity of the slight and pliant countertension together with the crisp rebound produces a special kind of unhampered lightness which is different from that met with in any other physical action.

A movement can be considered as light when the effort of muscular relaxation prevails in it. This is the case in almost all "fine touch" actions, where the weight of the object is inconsiderable—for instance, flicking away dust. Fine touch actions besides flicking are light stirring, floating, wafting, gliding, light smoothing, light jerking, dabbing, tapping, and so on.

Physically, the slight motion of air and water, the hovering of a feather, are examples of light movements in which the pressure of weight is inconsiderable. The stirrings of the body in which no external weight has to be moved can all be performed in a relatively relaxed way and the sensation of relative weightlessness can be experienced.

3. Punching or Thrusting

punching or thrusting—is sudden, direct, firm.

Punching is best felt first by the hands and arms making a fist and thrusting vehemently and quickly in a straight line towards a target point. In the legs the punching action is experienced in stamping steps.

Punching should be performed in all directions round the body with one arm at a time, accompanied by thrusting with the leg of the same side, or the opposite side. It should later be felt in other parts of the body, such as the elbows, shoulders, hips, knees, and head.

The main zone in which punching is usefully exercised with the arms lies across the body and backwards deep. To perform this action in the zone indicated directly necessitates a strong concentration of the whole body. The accompanying stamping step is to be made first on the spot and later in any desired direction.

There are endless possibilities of punching, e.g. with one arm separately, or both together, downwards, upwards, across, sideways, forwards, and backwards, moving into all directions of space, not only away from the body, but also towards it. Other possible variations are punching simultaneously with the arms in different directions, or punching with different parts of the body in various directions—for example, hips sideways, while one or both arms thrust upwards, and so on.

The legs can punch into the air in many directions or

can make the above-mentioned stamping steps. Leg-punching into the air and in steps can be combined with punching of any of the upper parts of the body in any direction.

Punching can be performed standing, sitting, kneeling, or lying, and lead to any change of position.

If a real object is the target of a punch, a natural resistance is encountered. Punching without having an object as a target needs a counter-tension of antagonist muscles. If this set of muscles did not co-operate, one would fall or be thrown in the direction of the punch. This counter-tension is to be felt in the whole body, so that even in punching with the forearm and fist only, an alertness and strength are felt in the legs, trunk, and neck. The stance must be firm.

"Fighting against" Weight, Space, and Time (without any "indulging in"), which is the essence of punching, develops a valuable effort control and gives an entirely different movement experience from that gained by doing simple exercises of quick and strong tension. The elasticity of the direct and quick counter-tensions produces a special kind of energetic suddenness which is different from that met with in any other physical action.

A movement can be considered as quick when the effort of an abrupt or sudden muscular function prevails in it. Quick actions besides punching are—flicking, hitting, slashing, dabbing, jerking, thrusting, *et cetera*.

Physically, this abrupt character of a sudden motion is to be found in explosions or in the released jerk of a spring. Bodily actions of quickness cannot be prolonged without losing their character. A punch, when slowed down, becomes a sustained pressure.

Quick actions can be repeated at longer or shorter intervals, but will themselves always have a short duration.

4. Floating or Flying

floating or flying—is sustained, flexible, light.

This action can most easily be felt while flying through the air in a leap.

It can also be experienced in the slight stir of the resting body when gently following the movement of respiration, say from a lying position as if awakening.

Floating movements can be directed into various zones of space, the most important being on the open side and forwards high, but there are endless possibilities, e.g. with each arm separately, or both together, floating downwards, upwards, across, sideways, forwards, and backwards, moving in all directions of space.

Floating should also be experienced in other parts of the body, such as the shoulders, elbows, chest, head, hips, knees, legs, and feet, not only extending into space away from the body, but also towards it.

Other possible variations are floating simultaneously with both arms in different directions, or floating with different parts of the body in various directions; for example, the body and steps floating or flying forwards, while arms go backwards, and so on.

The legs can float or fly into the air in many directions, or floating steps can be performed in touching the floor lightly on tiptoes. Such steps can be combined with floating movements of any of the upper parts of the body in any direction of space.

Floating can be performed in standing, kneeling, sitting, or lying positions. Floating movements can serve as transitions during changes between the various positions of the body.

Floating movements can be made in relation to specific objects or practical actions, say in lightly stirring a liquid. In this case resistance is offered by the object. Floating or stirring without relation to an external object, say hovering in the air during a flying leap, involves tensions in special sets of muscles which help to overcome the weight of the body or of the floating limb. Keeping these tensions as slight as possible increases the experience of sustainment felt in the whole body, feet, legs, trunk, *et cetera*.

"Indulging in" Time, Weight, and Space (without any "fighting against"), which is the essence of floating, develops a valuable effort control and gives an entirely different movement experience from that gained by doing simple exercises of slow movements. The slight and multilateral counter-tensions produce a special kind of gentle sustainment which is different from that met with in any other physical action.

A movement can be considered as sustained when the effort of continuous muscular function prevails in it. Sustained actions besides floating are—pressing, wringing, gliding, and their derivatives, such as pulling, smoothing, and so on.

Physically, floating, say in the hovering of smoke, is sustained in contrast to the abruptness of a spark. Continuity of a muscular action can have a shorter or longer duration, but the action will never be sudden.

5. Wringing

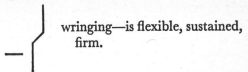

wringing—is flexible, sustained, firm.

Wringing can vary from a pulling to a twisting movement, and is felt more easily in the shoulders, arms, and hands than in the hips and legs. The feeling of strength must not be lost, as the slow muscular resistance felt in pressing is also present in this effort, but wringing produces a different sensation as the joints move more flexibly.

At first, wringing should be felt in the hands, as in wringing out clothes, and then extended, using different parts of the body. The whole body can be set into a wringing motion, for example, in a yawning stretch.

Wringing movements of the arms can be directed into various zones, the most important as far as exercises are concerned being on the open side and forwards deep, but there are many possibilities, e.g. with each arm separately, or both together, wringing downwards, upwards, across, sideways, forwards, and backwards, moving in all directions of space.

Wringing should also be experienced in other parts of the body, such as the shoulders, trunk, hips, legs, not only extending into space away from the body, but also towards it. Other possible variations are wringing simultaneously with both arms in different directions, or wringing with different parts of the body in various directions; for example, wringing the trunk in a backwards bending movement and doing the same action with arms sideways high, *et cetera*.

Wringing gestures can be made by the legs in preparing steps, and the wringing can be continued in performing the actual steps, i.e. screwing the foot into the floor as the body weight is transferred on to it. Wringing can be performed in any position—standing, kneeling, sitting, or lying—and can be a transitional movement during a change from one position to another.

In wringing out a cloth or twining several ropes together, resistance is offered by the object. Wringing of the body or of parts of it, without any object, calls certain additional sets of muscles into play, which operate the necessary counter-twist. A strong tension is thus produced, which can extend throughout the whole body, so that even when wringing with the hands alone there is counter-tension in the legs, trunk, and neck, giving an experience of controlled flexibility.

"Indulging in" Space and Time, and "fighting against" Weight, which is the essence of wringing, develops a valuable effort control and gives an entirely different movement experience from that gained by doing simple twisting exercises. The continuous firmness of the counter-tensions produces a special kind of sustained flexibility which is different from that met within any other physical action.

A movement can be considered as flexible when the effort of multilateral muscular function prevails in it. This effort brings about continuous changes of the direction of the movement. Flexible actions besides wringing are—slashing, floating, flicking, and some of their derivatives.

Physically, whirls and eddies of air and water, or the agitation of flames, might show flexible motions. Bodily actions of flexible character show the simultaneous pull of various muscle-groups in different directions. Complicated directional changes resulting in a twisted movement pattern assist the character of flexible actions.

6. Dabbing

dabbing—is direct, sudden, light.

This action is felt most easily in the hands in a light movement, such as that of a painter dabbing on spots of colour, or in the fingers as in typewriting. It can be felt in the legs in quick pointing of the feet or quick padding movements up and down.

Dabbing should be experienced first in the hands in all possible directions and then in the feet and legs. It can also be felt in the shoulders and in quick movements of the head.

Dabbing can be performed by the hands in any direction, but a very useful one is dabbing across the body over the opposite shoulder backwards and up. There are endless possibilities of dabbing, e.g. with each hand separately, or both together, dabbing downwards, upwards, across, sideways, forwards, and backwards, moving in all directions of space.

Dabbing should also be experienced in parts of the body other than in the hands and feet. Shoulders, elbows, chin, head, knees can dab, but also the larger parts of the body, such as the hips, chest, and back, can perform dabbing movements.

It is possible to dab not only in moving into space away from the body, but also towards it. Other possible variations are dabbing simultaneously with both hands in different directions, or dabbing with different parts of the body in various directions, for example, dabbing with a foot on the floor and with one or both hands upwards, and so on.

The legs can dab into the air in many directions or make dabbing or tapping steps, and these can be combined with dabs of the upper parts of the body. Dabbing can be performed standing, kneeling, sitting, or lying, and dabbing movements can be used in order to move from one position to another.

In dabbing at an object, resistance is felt. In dabbing in the air, the resistance is produced by special sets of muscles. The characteristic resiliency of this action becomes obvious in repeated dabs, as in shaking parts of the body. Shaking or vibrating consists of several dabs with elastic counter-tension. Shaking, and even a single dab, can have a repercussion in the whole body, so that even in dabbing with one finger only there can be felt counter-tension in the trunk, legs, neck, *et cetera*, producing an experience of controlled directness.

"Fighting against" Space and Time connected with "indulging in" Weight (shown in a certain relaxation and feeling of lightness), which is the essence of dabbing, develops a valuable effort control and gives an entirely different movement experience from that gained by doing simple straight line exercises. The alert fineness of grip in the counter-tensions, together with the elastic rebound, produces a special kind of sudden directness which is different from that encountered in any other physical action.

A movement can be considered as direct when the effort of unilateral muscular function prevails in it.

Direct actions other than dabbing are—gliding, punching, thrusting, pressing, *et cetera*.

Physically, falling, shooting, streaming, show a kind
of canalisation in space which is an example of direct
motion.

In bodily actions of great directness all active muscle-
groups co-operate in producing, as a rule, a well-traced
pattern having no plasticity.

Muscle-groups which are unsuitable to support the
intended direction remain passive; that means they are
not ready to function.

7. Slashing

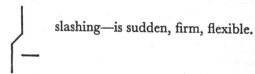

slashing—is sudden, firm, flexible.

This action has such variations as whipping, which is
less strong, or beating, which is less flexible; both show
also a decreased fluency. Slashing can be experienced
most easily in one arm at a time, beginning forwards,
high across the body, and ending deep backwards and
open, and then in the legs by standing on one and
slashing with the free leg outwards.

At first the slashing should be experienced in all
directions round the body with each arm separately,
and then with each leg.

There are endless possibilities of slashing into many
zones and directions, e.g. with each arm separately, or
both together, slashing downwards, upwards, across,
sideways, forwards, and backwards, moving in all
space directions.

Slashing should also be experienced in parts of the body other than arms and legs, such as shoulders, elbows, hips, knees, feet, and also head.

Slashing with the feet only will be near to flicking, but stronger. Slashing can be performed not only moving into space away from the body, but also towards it.

Other possibilities are slashing simultaneously with both arms, each in different directions, or slashing with different parts of the body in various directions; for example, one knee slashing diagonally high across the body and the opposite shoulder diagonally deep in the opposite direction, and so on.

Legs can slash into the air, but might also perform slashing steps, especially in jumping. Such slashing jumps and steps can be combined with slashing movements in the upper part and extremities of the body.

Slashing can be performed in standing, kneeling, sitting, or lying positions, and slashing movements can be made as transitions from one such position to another.

In slashing at something concrete, the object offers resistance to the action, but in slashing through the air, the movement has an extraordinary freedom of fluency which must be checked by definite sets of muscles. If these muscles did not co-operate, a strong slashing movement would throw the body off balance in an uncontrolled curve. Such slashing impulses can be used to perform large turning jumps, *et cetera*. Well-performed slashing gives the feeling of a free flow of movement.

"Fighting against" Weight and Time connected with "indulging in" Space, which is the essence of slashing, develops a valuable effort control and gives an entirely different movement experience from that gained by doing simple throwing and jumping exercises. The nimble adjustment of the strong and multi-lateral counter-tensions developed in slashing produces a special kind of flexible fluency which is different from that met with in any other physical action.

A movement can be considered as fluent or showing free flow when the effort of stopping is almost entirely absent. Fluent actions besides slashing, which mostly fades out into floating, are flicking, drifting, wafting, flying, even thrusting when its impulse fades into gliding. Some of these actions can, however, be performed in both ways, with free or with bound flow.

Physically, streaming, flowing, and parts of ballistic actions have fluent motions. The muscles antagonistic to the fluent character of the action remain passive, without readiness to function.

8. Gliding

gliding—is sustained, light, direct.

This action can be felt most easily in the palms of the hands, as if they were moving over a smooth surface; and then in the legs by standing on one and sliding the sole of the free foot lightly over the floor.

At first one can experience this effort by gliding with the palms facing downwards and moving them parallel with the floor in all directions round the body, and then in an up-and-down direction, with the palms facing forward. These gliding actions can be accompanied by walking steps, which should also be smooth and executed in a gliding manner.

Gliding with the trunk alone is difficult, but the

sensation of gliding should be felt in the body as well as in the hands and legs, for instance, in a smooth bowing or swaying movement.

Gliding of hands can be directed into various zones, the most important being across the body and high forwards, but there are endless possibilities, e.g. with each hand separately, or both together, gliding downwards, upwards, across, sideways, forwards, and backwards, extending in all directions of space. Gliding should also be experienced in other parts of the body, such as the shoulders, elbows, head, chest, back, hips, knees, and feet, not only moving into space away from the body, but also towards it.

Other possible variations are gliding simultaneously with both hands in different directions, or gliding with different parts of the body in various directions; for example, one hip gliding diagonally forwards, the opposite shoulder moving with the same action in a counter-direction, and so on.

The legs can glide into the air or in gliding steps along the floor. Gliding steps can be connected with gliding gestures of other parts of the body. Gliding can be performed in standing, kneeling, sitting, or lying positions, and it is possible to connect one position with another by a gliding movement.

In gliding along something, resistance is offered by the object. In gliding through the air with no object involved, definite sets of muscles enter into play in order to provide the counter-tension, which can be felt throughout the whole body. These counter-tensions give the feeling of controlled boundness.

"Indulging in" Weight and Time, and "fighting against" Space, which is the essence of gliding, develops a valuable effort control and gives an entirely different movement experience from that gained by doing simple exercises of, say, soft bending and stretching. The sustained gentleness of the unilateral pull of the counter-tensions produces a special kind of direct boundness which is different from that encountered in any other physical action.

A movement can be considered as bound when its prevailing effort is the readiness to stop. Apart from gliding, other actions tending to be rather bound are those of pressing, wringing, thrusting, pushing, pulling, and so on.

Physically, the stretching or compressing of resilient objects is an example of bound motion.

The bodily means of performing bound movements is the participation of antagonistic muscles which help in the steady control of an action.

Anybody who has tried to experience in his own body the eight basic effort actions described here will have become aware of the possibility of performing several of these in a coherent sequence.

EFFORT RHYTHMS

It is in fact very seldom that an isolated effort action is produced without any connection or relationship with others either preceding or following it. Almost any work-operation or expressive gesture shows the following pattern: preparation—one or several main efforts—termination.

Such sequences or rhythms of effort can also be studied experimentally. In the following, certain essential types of effort rhythms are described.

Pressing—Gliding

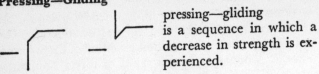

pressing—gliding
is a sequence in which a
decrease in strength is experienced.

It is obvious that the reversed form:

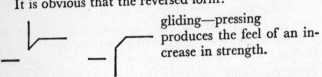

gliding—pressing
produces the feel of an increase in strength.

Such increase or decrease is felt most intensely when
both effort actions are performed with the same part of
the body. It is, however, possible to perform the first
effort of the sequence with one part of the body, say,
a stepping leg, and the second effort with another part
of the body, say, one of the palms and arms.

A pressing step resolving into a gliding arm gesture is
one of the numerous experiments which can be made.

In principle it is possible to combine any of the
described variations of pressing (Section 1) with any of
the variations of gliding (Section 8).

The effort rhythm of these combinations will be
sustained—sustained; it must be realised, however,
that in relation to a metrical beat one of the two
combined actions might be of shorter duration than the
other:

pressing	—	gliding
(relatively long)	—	(relatively short,
		but never sudden)
pressing	—	gliding
(relatively short,		(relatively long)
but never sudden)		

Relative length of duration and relative shortness of duration can be in any proportion to one another.

Other action combinations of the same effort rhythm

besides: are:

and in reverse sequence.

Floating—Flicking

floating—flicking
differ in the Time element, and an increase in speed will therefore be felt in the performance of this sequence.

The reverse:

flicking—floating
leading from suddenness to sustainment, will give the experience of a decrease in speed.

Both efforts, together forming a sequence, can be performed by the same or by different parts of the body in any direction or combination of directions of space.

Any variation described in Section 2 can be combined with any variation described in Section 4.

The effort rhythm of these combinations will be either:

sustained—sudden

or

sudden—sustained.

Flicking will be more abrupt than floating. Floating of a very short duration will be scarcely distinguishable from a pause. This refers, of course, to any action in which the Time element is sustained; as the sustainment can be prolonged practically to any extent, the duration of the sustained action can be any multiple of the duration of a sudden and quick action.

A pressing, gliding, wringing, or floating action of the same duration as a sudden one will be felt almost as a hiatus or slight pause in a movement sequence and it will also be perceived as such by a spectator.

Other action combinations of the above effort rhythms

besides: are:

and in reverse sequence.

Punching—Slashing

punching—slashing is a sequence in which the change from directness to flexibility can be most intensely felt.

The opposite is the case in the reversed form of this sequence.

These sequences can be performed by the same or by different parts of the body in any direction or combination of directions in space.

Any variation described under Section 3 can be combined with any variation described under Section 7.

The effort rhythm of these combinations is:

sudden—sudden.

In the metrical sense of rhythm there will be no difference of duration between the two efforts constituting the sequence, because sudden actions cannot be essentially increased or decreased in duration.

Other action combinations of the same effort rhythm

besides: are:

and in reverse sequence.

Any other combination of two or more efforts forming a sequence or rhythm is possible. They will be characterised by changes of two or all three of the basic effort elements. Closer scrutiny shows that if they seem to melt into one another, there will always be a pause, sometimes almost imperceptible, between them, or a very short transitional effort. For instance, in combining pressing with floating the following transitions are frequent:

Any of the basic effort actions described under Sections 1 to 8 can be combined with any other. When they differ in more than one effort element, transitional efforts will be detectable between them. The experiencing of transitional effort is an essential part of experimental effort study as a basis of a free dance technique.

APPLIED COMBINATIONS

Certain combinations of effort actions occur in everyday occupations, sports, and other physical activities.

The throwing of a ball or a stone is a combined action, possibly starting with a floating, followed by a thrust which might be dissolved into gliding. Whisking is a combination of flicking in which the increased weight element develops the effort of slashing. Serving in tennis may be done by a sequence of flick—float—slash, while bowling on a green may contain a float—

glide combination. The efforts of such sequences melt into one another with almost imperceptible transitions.

COUPLES AND GROUPS

Response to the actions of another person or group of people can be simultaneous with, or occur just after, the movement of the opposing partner or group, as an answering action.

First person or group		Second person or group
press	against	wring
slash	,,	flick
thrust	,,	float

either simultaneously or one after the other.

The actions can be accompanied by steps, and the responses may take the form of leaps or turns—so that the persons, couples, or groups create a floor pattern, for example:

One person or group can step forward and thrust, while the other responds by a slashing turn.

Other variations in reaction can be felt when the opposing groups or couples use different parts of the body.

One group may make the first movement using their legs chiefly, to which the other group responds by using their arms.

Several persons or groups may respond to each other, for example, one using the efforts "float and press" against a "dab and slash," while a third does "punch and glide."

Other responses arise when one person or group begins with gradually accelerating movement, while the opposing person or group sinks slowly to the ground; or one person or group may approach with a turn and leap while the other responds by calmly kneeling or sitting. All examples can be carried out with the movements consisting of a single action or a combination of actions.

Group reactions may be improvised, that is, they may arise spontaneously, or as a reaction to some stimulus such as music, words, dramatic situations, movement of others, *et cetera*.

They may also be carefully preconsidered, or composed, so that each group is clearly aware of the changes from one action to another.

It is valuable to repeat group reactions in order to train movement memory, so that the dancers learn to repeat a dance sequence without a mental effort.

DERIVATIVES

The basic effort actions have derivatives which arise through a special emphasis being given to one element.

In the graphs the accent is indicated by a dot added to the stroke representing the stressed element:

Pressing:

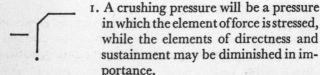

1. A crushing pressure will be a pressure in which the element of force is stressed, while the elements of directness and sustainment may be diminished in importance.

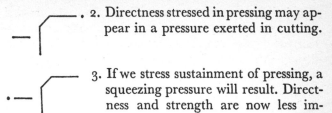

2. Directness stressed in pressing may appear in a pressure exerted in cutting.

3. If we stress sustainment of pressing, a squeezing pressure will result. Directness and strength are now less important.

Flicking: simple derivatives can also be found in flicking as characterised by the actions of flipping flicks, flapping and jerking flicks.

Slashing: derivatives of slashing are a beating slash, throwing and whipping slashes.

Dabbing: has derivatives such as patting, tapping, shaking dabs.

Wringing: in this effort through the stressing of single elements, derivatives can be found, such as stretching, pulling, plucking wrings.

Gliding: has derivatives such as smoothing, smearing (painting), smudging glides.

Punching: has derivatives such as shoving, thrusting, poking, piercing punches.

Floating: is changed through stress of elements into strewing, stirring, stroking floats.

Some action verbs will express exaggerations of basic or derivative effort actions, as for instance groping, fumbling, disentangling, kicking, breaking, dragging, hurrying, *et cetera.*

Other action terms represent very simple efforts in which only one element is important. For example, falling, rising, growing, shrinking, penetrating, stiffening, *et cetera.*

The smallest muscle action, even the twitching of a face muscle or almost imperceptible finger movement, shows the same action qualities and significance as large movements.

The teacher of free dance should be aware of the quality of any of the large or small movements used in dance compositions.

CHAPTER V

THE CONCEPTION OF THE SPHERE OF MOVEMENT*

ALL movement takes place by transferring the body or parts of the body from one position in space to another. Accordingly, each movement is partly explicable from these spatial changes of position. Using generally accepted terms of our language we can describe the exact point from which a movement starts; in the same manner we can define the point to which a movement leads or at which it arrives. The joining of the two points is the "path" along which the movement travels.

Wherever the body moves or stands, it is surrounded by space. Around the body is the "sphere of movement," or "*Kin*esphere," the circumference of which can be reached by normally extended limbs without changing one's stance, that is, the place of support. The imaginary inner wall of this sphere can be touched by hands and feet, and all points of it can be reached.

Outside this immediate sphere lies the wider or "general" space which man can enter only by moving away from the original stance. He has to step outside the borders of his immediate sphere and create a new one from the new stance, or, in other words, he transfers what might be called his "personal" sphere to another place in the general space. Thus, in actual fact, he never goes outside his personal sphere of movement, but carries it around with him like a shell.

* A detailed exposition of this is given by the author in his book, *Choreutics*.

So, when a man makes several steps forward, he carries his sphere of movement forward into the general space for the distance of his steps. For him his stance is always "below," never "in front." He is immediately aware of the new stance as the basis of his sphere, and from it he builds his next movements.

The following movement experiments will prove to be useful.

Division of space

As a simple means of orientation in space we know three dimensions. Each one of the three dimensions has:

a Direction	and	a Counter-direction
high (*h*)		deep (*d*)
right (*r*)		left (*l*)
forwards (*f*)		backwards (*b*)

In relation to our body we have the feeling that these directions and counter-directions irradiate from the centre of our sphere of movement in which the three dimensions intersect one another. Spatially these dimensional directions present themselves to us as a flat cross *h*—*d* and *l*—*r* through the centre of which runs the line *b*—*f*, thus forming a three-dimensional cross:

This three-dimensional cross can be placed into an imaginary cube within one's personal sphere where its centre coincides with those of the cube and body. From this centre and between the dimensions run oblique lines towards the corners of the cube. We call them diagonal directions. There are four space "diagonals" leading from one corner of the cube to its opposite. They intersect one another in the centre of the sphere of movement, so that in each diagonal we can recognise:

a Direction	and	a Counter-direction
high right forwards (*hrf*)		deep left backwards (*dlb*)
high left forwards (*hlf*)		deep right backwards (*drb*)
high right backwards (*hrb*)		deep left forwards (*dlf*)
high left backwards (*hlb*)		deep right forwards (*drf*)

In order to get a more differentiated division of space than that which is obtained by dividing it into dimensional directions and diagonals, we can imagine further directions which are neither dimensional nor diagonal. From the centre and between two dimensional and two diagonal directions run oblique lines towards the central point of the cube edges. Their directions we call "diametral" directions.

There are six diameters which intersect one another in the centre of the sphere of movement and in each diameter we can recognise:

a Direction	and	a Counter-direction
high right (*hr*)		deep left (*dl*)
right forwards (*rf*)		left backwards (*lb*)
deep forwards (*df*)		high backwards (*hb*)
deep right (*dr*)		high left (*hl*)
right backwards (*rb*)		left forwards (*lf*)
deep backwards (*db*)		high forwards (*hf*)

Therefore, briefly summarising the division of space thus created in relation to an imaginary cube within our personal sphere of movement, we can discern the three-dimensional cross which radiates from the centre to the central points of the surfaces of the cube. The four diagonals connect the opposite corner points of the cube, while the six diameters are directed towards the edges of the cube which they bisect. All these twenty-six space-directions radiate from the space-centre, which is the twenty-seventh point of orientation. See Fig. 2, Chapter IV (p. 37).

Paths in personal space

The division of space related to the moving body will show that each limb can move from any of the twenty-seven points of orientation to any other point. The movements will follow either straight paths or slightly curved ones. The latter will essentially be the case when the position of the points demands a circumvention of the body which stands between them.

For example, the path from b to f cannot be performed by an arm in a direct way, because the body is situated between b and f (in c). The arm must therefore go round the body, as near as possible to it, of course, so that the main direction is kept. All paths going through the centre must be performed along such slightly curved lines.

Other paths, as for instance b to r or r to f, can be performed by the right hand and arm in a straight line, because there is no obstacle in between. All paths which do not go through the centre can, but need not, be performed along straight lines. In fluent movements man has the habit of smoothing out the corners by using slightly curved movements, which differ from

THE CONCEPTION OF THE SPHERE OF MOVEMENT 89

angular movements consisting of a combination of straight lines or those accentuating the orientation points sharply.

Some fundamental patterns will be easily recognised. Movements connecting two points form a line:

$$lb—rf$$
$$lb—hf$$
$$lb—hl$$

Movements connecting three points form an angle:

$$lb—rf—db$$
$$lb—hf—dr$$
$$lb—hl—hb$$

Movements connecting three points and returning to the starting point form a triangle:

$$lb—rf—db—lb$$
$$lb—hf—dr—lb$$
$$lb—hl—hb—lb$$

Movements connecting four points and returning to the starting point form a quadrangle:

$$lb—hf—rf—db—lb$$
$$lb—lf—rf—rb—lb$$

In returning to the starting point after a series of any desired number of points, a closed line is performed. Closed lines or circuits can be performed fluently, that is, with smooth directional transition as well as angularly, that is, with accentuated and sharp transitions. A closed line or circuit connecting all dimensional points is, for example:

$$l—h—b—r—d—f—l$$

It forms a six-link circuit along edges of an octa-hedron. There exist several such edge lines inter-linking all dimensional points. A closed line or circuit connecting all diagonal points is, for example:

hrf—drf—dlf—hlf—hlb—dlb—drb—hrb—hrf

It forms an eight-link circuit along edges of a cube. There exist several such edge lines interlinking all diagonal points. A closed line or circuit connecting all diametral points is, for example:

hr—rf—df—dr—rb—bd—dl—lb—hb—hl—lf—hf—hr

It forms a twelve-link circuit along edges of a cube-octahedron. There exist several such edge lines inter-linking all diametral points which we shall call "primary circuits."

All primary circuits of the twelve diametral points show an order in the spatial relations of each point to any other. This can be determined by the number of circuit links or intervals which lie between the points in question.

Movements can be performed along lines connecting any one point with any other, for example:

hr—rf
hr—df
hr—dr   et cetera.

Movements connecting points of the primary circuit which are a distance of four links or intervals away from one another form equilateral triangles. For example, in moving from the first point of the above-mentioned circuit to the fifth, ninth, and finally back to the first, the following triangle is performed:

hr—rb—hb—hr

Movements connecting points of the primary circuit which are a distance of three links or intervals away from one another form regular squares. For example, in moving from the first point of the above-mentioned circuit to the fourth, seventh, tenth, and finally back to the first one, the following square is performed:

$$hr—dr—dl—hl—hr$$

Starting at any one point on the circuit, the movements over the distances of four intervals will always form triangular circuits, and over distances of three intervals will always form quadrangular circuits.

Movements over distances of five intervals perform a star-like chain of twelve links which makes a circuit within the cube-octahedron. Therefore, each link traverses the kinesphere yet clearly avoids the centre. For instance, in moving several times along the primary circuit starting at the first point and proceeding to its sixth — eleventh — fourth — ninth — second — seventh — twelfth — fifth — tenth — third — eighth and finally first one again, the following star-like chain is performed, which is of great importance for the exercise of harmonious movement:

$$hr—db—lf—dr—hb—rf—dl—hf—rb—hl—df—lb—hr$$

Zones of limbs

In performing such paths in space, or parts of them, or any other shape of movement connecting whichever points one might choose, first by the right and afterwards by the left arm, one will find in some cases less, and in others more difficulty. Some movements can be performed only with considerable contortions of the body. There is, however, no sequence

or combination which could not be performed if the
trunk is appropriately bent and twisted and the legs are
sufficiently flexed or stretched. Such movements
should be done without turning, which means without
changing the position of the feet. In each movement
one of the feet must always retain or reoccupy this
initial position on its original stance.

To reach the highest points of the kinesphere with the
feet is an acrobatic feat which may be attempted but
cannot be attained without arduous training. The highest points normally to be reached by leg movements are
rf, rb, lf, lb. Those points which can easily be reached by
any one limb outline the normal zone of that limb. A
right or a left arm zone can therefore be distinguished
as well as a right or left leg zone. To be able to increase
the extent of zones is a sign of a higher degree of
mobility.

Pathways through general space

The transfer of the sphere of movement from one
place to another by any desired number of steps can
lead along straight lines or curved paths. One can also
jump, and thus transfer the sphere of movement to a
new place.

When jumping on the spot, with the arms reaching
far in the dimensional direction of h, or in the
diametral directions of hr and hl simultaneously, they
seem to reach beyond the kinesphere but in fact the
personal sphere of movement is momentarily elevated
above the ground. Jumps into diametral and diagonal
directions lead both to elevating the sphere off the
ground and to pathways through general space. After
each jump a new stance or place is reached.

The sphere of movement can not only be transferred; it can also be turned in relation to the outer surroundings. After half a turn one's front and therefore all the *f* directions (*f*, *rf*, *lf*, *df*, *hrf*, *lhf*, *drf*, *dlf*) will now be orientated towards that area into which all *b* directions formerly led.

In a full turn all one's *f* directions regain the same relation to the surrounding space as they had before the turn.

With turning jumps a transfer and a change of front of the sphere of movement can be performed simultaneously.

Movements in all directions, as well as sequences of directions, can be performed with different extensions; normal, when the directions involved in the movement are pursued within easy reach of the active parts of the body; narrow or small, when the extent is less than half its normal; wide or large, when exaggerated stretching is used.

The centre *c* is a directional aim like any other point. It is frequently the starting point, but it can also be included in a sequence of directions.

The body centre is carried away in transfers of the sphere of movement by steps or jumps, but apart from that it can be lowered, which leads to the bending of knees, crouching, kneeling, sitting, and lying.

The direction *c* is always in the body centre. In crouching while directing the arms towards *c*, a very concentrated form of the sphere of movement is created.

Movements along a line, or circuits of directional sequences, can be performed either fluently or angularly. In fluent performance more stress will normally be laid on the paths, and in angular performance on the points.

Any transfer of the body or of parts of it from one position in space to another takes time. Accordingly, each movement is, apart from its shape, characterised by the length or stretch of time which it takes. We can establish the relation of the time taken for a movement to the time taken by another one preceding or following it. We call this relation the time-rhythm of the movement. A rhythm consists of two or more time stretches of consecutive movements. They can be of equal or different length.

The movement begins with the departure from one point in space and continues via one or several more until the terminal one is reached. Each stretch between the points takes a certain length or stretch of time. When the movement is stopped its journey through space and time has come to an end.

The start of a new movement leads through further stretches of space and time to the next stop. A stop interrupts the movement in space but its duration in time can become part of the rhythmical development of a movement sequence and can be measured in relation to the preceding and succeeding time stretches of the movement in space.

Any movement is characterised by two factors: the shape created by stretches of space and the rhythms created by stretches of time, both performed by the body or by parts of it.

The path between three or more points in space characterises the shape of a movement. In some stretches of it, particularly in those where there is a marked change of direction, an increase of muscular exertion can be noticed which provides the accents in the phrase.

Accents give a certain weight to some phases within the shape of a movement. Accentuated or stressed movements can be considered as strong, while the unstressed ones are light.

The combined elements of Weight and Time become evident in musical rhythms. The element of Space as shown by the shapes of movement is in this case subordinated to the musical rhythm. Here the Time element is used in a highly differentiated manner. The musical notation of rhythm can be used by the dancer, but so also can the prosodic notation of rhythm as used in poetry.

Rhythm is, however, only a part of music, a kind of skeleton around which the main content of the musical composition, the melodies and harmonies of tones, is built. In dance accompaniment the melody and harmony of tones often recede and the importance of rhythm increases. Purely rhythmic instruments, such as drums and other percussion instruments, are used for the production of audible rhythms without melodies or harmonies of tone.

Rhythmic music is an incentive to rhythmic movement, but it is only when a fully developed flow of movement, including a definite composition of shapes and effort shadings, has been built up around the rhythm, that one can speak of dance proper.

The modern dancer often composes the shape and effort flow of movement first and adapts the accompanying audible rhythm or music to his movement invention. Dances without any accompaniment are possible, and have been successfully performed. The interpretation of musical compositions which have not been created for dancing has a short-lived popularity. Valuable dances very rarely arise from such interpretation.

One effort element may appear in a movement in such an intensive form that the two others are completely overshadowed. It may happen that a movement impresses us mainly as strong or light, because neither its Space quality nor its Time quality is stressed in any way. It may also happen that two elements are stressed and the third one is irrelevant. Such "incomplete actions" appear frequently as transitions between main efforts.

In conclusion, it can be said that a movement may be described as a composite of its shapes and rhythms, both being part of the superposed flow of movement in which the effort control exerted by the moving person becomes visible.

There are unlimited variations of dance phrases which can be made from different combinations of the eight effort actions, together with variations of leg gestures, steps, leaps, and turns along different floor patterns and space directions. These phrases should at first be simple, and only gradually be developed into more complex forms. They may comprise any imaginable combination of movements as used in the art of movement and in everyday life activities.

Dance styles of all times and all countries contain such movement combinations, and many new forms can be invented.

A better understanding of historical dances can be gained through studying their content of basic effort actions and exact space directions.

CHAPTER VI

THE OBSERVATION OF MOVEMENT

A REFRESHING swim in the sea is a wonderful and health-giving thing, but no human being could live constantly in the water. It is a very similar case with the occasional swim in the flow of movement which we call dance. Such swimming, refreshing in many respects for the body, the mind, and for that dreamy part of our being which has been called the soul, is an exceptional pleasure and stimulation. As water is a widespread means of sustaining life, so is the flow of movement.

It is perhaps worth while to advance this simile a little farther, because this can save us many long explanations. Water is in our veins, in our food. Water cleanses our body and our surroundings. Water is a means of transport by supplying our engines with steam, and our ships sail on water.

The flow of movement fills all our functions and actions; it discharges us of detrimental inner tensions; it is a means of communication between people, because all our forms of expression, such as speaking, writing, and singing are carried by the flow of movement.

Dance, understood as a total immersion in the flow of movement, brings us thus into a more intensive contact with a medium which carries and permeates all our activities. It is obvious, therefore, that the educational value of dance is partly due to the universality with which the flow of movement is used in our life and partly to the act of total immersion in its medium, the flow of movement. The advantages of the first kind offered by dance are material; practice of the use of the flow of movement will enable the child to employ his mobility for all practical purposes in everyday life. This help is accentuated by the fact that man uses the same forms of movement in dance as in work, though they are arrayed in a different manner. Instead of objects being carried, the body is carried through space, and, while in work objects are hit and pressed and wrung, in dance we do the hitting, pressing, and wringing for their own sake. In dancing, the child practises the fluent performance of many bodily actions which have their use in everyday practical pursuits; thus he receives a valuable preparation for the different physical demands of life. The total immersion in an essential medium of life such as movement has the advantage of intensifying the experience of bodily actions which are practically useful.

Beyond this, however, there is something more profound in dance. As in all artistic activities, life experience is enhanced in dance through the concentration on definite rhythms and shapes of movement. The child becomes aware of the particularised entities of expression, and this is an indispensable pre-requisite of the clearness and exactitude of any kind of expression and communication between people.

The social value of dance is greatly determined by the peculiar attribute of this art, namely to make expression precise and, therefore, comprehensible for our fellowbeings. Not only the large movements which sometimes resemble working actions, but also all those finer shades of the smallest muscle actions, such as those of face or hands, are highly expressive and therefore communicative. An individual's preference for certain forms of movement, either consciously or unconsciously, reveals definite traits of his personality. Socially desirable traits of behaviour can be distinguished and more easily fostered by a teacher who has learnt how to observe and interpret movement.

We all think that we observe actions in others with sufficient accuracy to be able to understand and assess the people we observe, but in reality we are influenced by factors which distract us from what we actually see. Preconceived ideas, biased opinions, too-lively an imagination or too-ready censure, all obscure the only data we have—a person's movement as it was performed without reference to its result, whether productive, destructive, or communicative.

The movement, as it stands on its own, can be described in effort terms, without prejudice or criticism. This attitude is important for the teacher, who may see only one aspect of the children he handles, as he can guard against the dangers stated in connection with movement observation.

Teachers of all subjects will find this observation helpful when applied to their own movement, so that conflicting effort habits can be changed into more harmonious combinations. The teacher who is able to adjust his own efforts to those of the children with whom he works, has a great advantage in the accomplishment of his educational task.

A real understanding of the motion factors and of man's attitude towards them is necessary before the teacher can make use of his assessments for the benefit of either himself or the children. The different combinations of attitudes towards Space, Time, and Weight result in the various effort actions. People's capacity to make a balanced use of all of them varies considerably. More often than not a preponderance of a very limited range of effort expression can be observed, while the healthy human being has, at least to some degree, potential for an all-round development. Should only one type of effort combination be present, such as, for instance, thrusting, or slashing, in both of which the individual is fighting Time and Weight continuously, we shall find an unbalanced person with a lop-sided effort experience. Supposing a teacher has this characteristic, one often finds as a reaction that the natural efforts of the children become repressed and their attitude sullen or cowed. This is, of course, an extreme example of a conflict between the teacher's efforts and those of the class. In another case, a teacher with light, tentative, and hesitating movements might quickly be summed up by a class as being unsure of himself and his subject. Children have a natural perception of efforts and respond very quickly to these visible outward signs of their teacher's inner moods.

A teacher can learn to use an effort balance which is appropriate to the needs of the class, displaying firmness and bound control only when necessary, while the children feel free to experiment in their own way with effort combinations, thus increasing their effort experience and range.

Effort study should not only be the concern of teachers of physical activities, such as dance, gymnastics, or games; it is just as important to a teacher of academic subjects. Often even more so, as the child behind a desk is physically restricted and can usually let off steam only vocally, while in physically active lessons vital energy finds a natural outlet.

When we realise that movement is the essence of life, and that all expression, whether it be speaking, writing, singing, painting, or dancing, uses movement as a vehicle, we cannot help seeing the importance of understanding this outward expression of the living energy within, and this we can do through effort study. Let us suppose the teacher has acquired a working knowledge of this study and has applied it to himself. He is now ready to understand the spirit of the class he teaches, realising that the same effort components and combinations are present in both mental and bodily exertion. He must not accept the heavy apathetic mood of a dull class as inevitable, but try to stimulate its members into taking a more active attitude towards movement and effort. In dealing with a lively, excitable class, particular effort actions are needed; but the teacher will have to be aware of the existing mood, allow it sufficient scope and then gradually change the attitude of the class, through his own example.

The individual child in a class can be helped a great deal by a teacher who looks at his movements with an unprejudiced and understanding eye. A child whose movements are lethargic and heavy may not be lazy, but his attitude may be one of enjoying having time and indulging in it; he must be helped to adopt an active approach towards time by experiencing the effort actions of slashing, thrusting, dabbing, and flicking, which develop quickness and, by producing an unaccustomed sensation in the child, will help to adjust his effort balance.

We do not sufficiently realise the important effect action has on the mental state of the mover. Movement can inspire accompanying moods, which are felt more or less strongly according to the degree of effort involved.

Although there are only eight basic effort actions, a multitude of varying shades between these eight primary ones can be discerned, just as the primary colours can be blended to produce intermediary shades, combining two or more primary colours in varying degrees.

In watching a child we see his movements change from one effort to another, sometimes gradually in a harmonious way, sometimes abruptly and with no apparent connection with the previous movement. These changes, or mutations, are important, as they indicate the presence or absence of flow from one action, or state of mind, to the next. A harmonious change would be from a pressing to a gliding movement, as the attitudes to Time and Space elements are the same in both; only the attitude towards Weight is changed. The change from pressing to flicking involves a different attitude towards all three motion factors, and cannot be achieved without intermediary shades of effort. An abrupt change from one effort to its complete contrast indicates discord in the mental and bodily state of the child, but if this discord is understood, the child can be guided in such a way that he learns to make use of harmonious transitions from one effort to another.

It cannot be stressed too strongly that the movements the child experiences have a marked reaction on his mind, so that varying emotions can be induced through his actions, the intensity of the emotion varying with the intensity of the action. Small unconscious movements of the face and hands, or of isolated parts of the body, are as expressive of the child's mental state, and have as much effect on his mind, as larger movements, such as those carried out intentionally in an active lesson. It is therefore clearly apparent that a teacher confronted with a class behind desks can, through understanding, do as much to help the class as a whole, as well as each child individually, as a teacher of gymnastics or dance who is more immediately concerned with movement. An academic teacher should appreciate efforts expressed through movement, and a dance teacher has to realise that there is mental effort involved in all activity.

It is difficult to understand the full significance of movement and to observe accurately without long experience, but the teacher can begin by applying his knowledge to his own movements, analysing his efforts as accurately and dispassionately as possible.

The teacher's own "feelings" are, of course, not always reliable, and many movement habits are unconscious. It is easier to observe others than to correct oneself. A teacher who has enjoyed the best that present-day education can give may be surprised to find, after a thorough-going self-observation, his effort balance disturbed in such a way that he is, say, constantly fighting Time, with hurried, speedy movements; he may perpetually indulge in Space, with roundabout mental and bodily efforts, or he may be ponderous and heavy, enjoying his weightiness. These examples present a marked emphasis on one aspect of effort experience, which is harmful to the teaching individual and to the children whom he educates.

Future teachers' training should ensure that students

are prepared for life in such a way that they do not strive simply for intellectual success, or bodily skill, but that the various human efforts, the common denominator of mental and bodily activity, are more widely appreciated and used to develop their personality into an integrated whole. They will then be better equipped to educate children to become happy in themselves and in their relationship with others through the understanding of the basic manifestation of life—movement.

One who during his school days has not learnt to appreciate immersion in the universal flow of movement does not know that such a thing as a universal flow exists.

Education today endeavours to supply a counterbalance to this state of affairs by paying more attention to art education, and even dance has today re-entered the schools.

In the more complex forms of dancing, in which works of art are created and performed, the child learns to evaluate that higher synthesis of expression of which works of art consist. The opportunity to become acquainted with these forms of art arises either in individual dances or in group dances. In both cases the dancer is taken into an almost architectural whole of a movement composition which develops his taste; that means the faculty of judging larger groupings of events as a whole, instead of restricting his likes and dislikes to petty details of sensuous impressions. A group dance gives the child the experience of the adaptation of people to one another. Human relationships of a valuable kind can thus be promoted by group dancing.

In summarising, it can be said that the educative

value of dance is twofold: first, through the healthy mastery of movement, and secondly, through the enhancement of personal and social harmony promoted by exact effort observation.

It is, of course, possible to foster the healthy mastery of movement by other means than dancing. Physical exercise, games, and activities, including manual training, are the usual channels for achieving this aim. The enhancement of personal and social harmony is furthered by various subjects of education, which lack, however, that immediate personal experience which effort study and effort training give.

The lop-sided accent given to either bodily or mental experience of the flow of movement is an artificial procedure which might be useful for certain educative purposes. The undivided experience of the flow of movement in dancing answers an urge which all children and many adults feel. The urge to dance, to which all children without exception are subject from time to time, is ineradicable. I think the urge remains constant through life from the cradle to the grave in everybody, though it is frequently misinterpreted and perverted into sentiments and activities inadequate to fulfil the intended scope of developing effort-life, and with it, personality.

The teacher, therefore, needs a reliable guidance in the assessment of the content of dances and of their effect on the child. This is not simply an affair of taste or of the popularity of certain dance forms. On the whole, the bodily and mental food for children is fairly well controlled and selected. However, in the important field of the acquisition of action and effort habits by dancing no reliable selection is made. The children are fed either not at all, or with the stale remainders of the spirit of the past, entirely incompatible with the needs and knowledge of our days.

Through movement observation and analysis the teacher can acquire the necessary competence for judging the educational value of dance movements and dances. He or she will soon find that certain types of dance movements are apt to perpetuate innate and acquired effort deficiencies, while others offer the possibility of balancing discordant attitudes and of promoting a healthy growth of personality.

The study of dance movements, if it is to be of any value to education, must be based on a thorough knowledge of man's effort-life. The observation of the Weight, Time, Space, and Flow factors of movement, and of their combinations gives a clue to the means of conscious penetration into the jungle of dance forms and dance moods.

The schooled observer will soon notice that the pleasure given by dancing can surpass the physical satisfaction which is produced by the simple fact of exercising the body. Dance forms and dance exercises which induce the child to a mechanical performance of his movements belong to a different category from those which provide an outlet for the child's individual efforts. The latter convey more than the feel of regularly moved joints and muscles. The experience gained from the performance of definite actions, and the recognition of the rhythms contained in chains or sequences of actions, distinguish the more complex dance forms from the mechanical ones.

A clue to how the various dance forms could be classified may be found in the sixteen movement themes developed in Chapter III. The teacher will have to observe the effect of variations and combinations of these movement themes on individual children and groups of children. From this observation he or she will learn that a specific movement may have each time a similar impact on the child's mental and bodily attitude. Once a teacher has recognised such facts and collected a sufficient number of examples, the composition of such movement themes as are likely to further the child's development can be undertaken. To do this in a considered and considerate manner is an art in itself, which can be learnt only through long practice.

This is the way dance has been used for educational purposes throughout the whole history of mankind. Our time, however, has to find its own procedure, which must take into account the complex form of our present-day education, and the whole trend of our modern civilisation.

CHAPTER VII

SOME HINTS FOR THE STUDENT
OF MOVEMENT

Aims of dance in education

The material of dance is movement, by which in this context I mean the interaction of effort and space, as expounded by Laban, through the medium of the body. Our bodily movements make shapes in space and they are charged with effort, that is an energy coming from within, springing from a whole range of impulses, intentions, and desires. As we develop awareness of self and environment, we find that the body needs to be a sensitive instrument to make manifestation of the interplay between the inner and the outer world possible.

One of the aims of dance in education, and I think the most important one, is to help people through dancing to find bodily relation to the whole of existence. Dance is, as are all the arts, a source of knowledge which can be tapped, but we have to familiarise ourselves with its discipline and learn to perform its rhythms and forms distinctly, otherwise no benefit can be derived from it.

Laban has described in this book the gradual development of the movement capacity in children. A similar procedure would apply to adults who for the first time experience in themselves the liberation of the natural flow of movement. The aim, as Laban points out, "is the beneficial effect of the creative activity of dancing upon the personality" and not the production of sensational dances. The artifact is not an end in itself but a means through which artistic expression is fostered in a way that is both creative and appropriate to the gifts and stage of development of the pupils. In education, and also in recreation, we build up a dance experience on universal basic forms of movement and the subjective assimilation and reflection of these, and not on a conception of an outer presentation. Thus a movement vocabulary is gradually established which helps us to become expressive in the language of dance.

Why dance?

Movement, of course, is a feature of all man's activities. Why, then, do we think that dancing has a contribution to make to the preparation for living, which is the concern of education? In dance we are immersed in the action process itself, while in other activities, whether of sport or work, our attention is mostly engaged in the practical outcome of our actions. Although the movement sequences of all physical activities contain a specific effort of the mover, in the latter, awareness of the action process gives way to concentration on the external achievement. When we create and express in dance, when we perform and interpret its rhythms and forms, we are exclusively concerned with the handling of its material, which is movement itself. Through the movements of our body we can learn to relate our inner self to the outer world. We receive impressions from without to which we react, and we also project our spontaneous inner impulses outward, thus expressing the presence of life energy.

But it is not the mastery of isolated physical movements which enhances movement awareness. It is rather the reciprocal stimulation of the inward and outward flow of movement, pervading and animating the whole of the body, which is fostered in dancing.

It would, however, be wrong to assume that any kind of moving or jumping about, often called dancing, has the unifying and harmonising effect just described. Even the professional dancer does not often have the opportunity of experiencing this, as dancing is his job, which he has to fulfil in all circumstances no matter whether he derives a personal benefit from it or not.

Dancing, together with those artistic activities which are produced by the body as the sole instrument, such as miming, acting, singing, and speaking, is an aspect of the art of movement. Besides what it shares in common with the other arts, dance has its own body of knowledge, tradition, experience, historical development, and principles, which can be seen at work in the images created, in the methods of structuring used in bringing single movement forms into mutual relations, and in the styles developed.

Educating the sense of movement

The reader will have found in this book ample guidance in ways to build up his experience, knowledge, and creative faculty in movement, alongside the consideration of educational aims and methods. Of course, in an artistic activity this cannot be an intellectual process only, although the use of words tends to make it so. The explanatory statements represent solely a framework which has to be filled out and enlivened by an imagery based on a sensibility for movement. To develop the sense of movement, with which we all are endowed to a greater or lesser degree, is of paramount importance. For this a conscious awareness of motor sensations is necessary, combined with those arising from the interplay of effort and the body in space. Physical movements which are blurred in their effort rhythms, spatial forms, and bodily execution will neither enhance movement sensitivity nor the ability to create in movement. Knowledge of the organisation, and feel of the quality of the movement units, often freely and spontaneously created, need to be perfected, so that our bodily actions become specific enough to impress themselves on us, and a psycho-physical experience of movement is gained.

We are not all endowed with an equally fine kinaesthetic sense, that is the sense by which we perceive muscular effort, movement, and position in space. Its organs are not situated in any one particular part of the body, as those of seeing or hearing, for instance, but they are nerve endings embedded in muscular fibres all over the body. Through musical sound we try to refine our sense of hearing; through the interplay of colours and shapes in art we try to refine our sense of seeing; and through dancing we try to refine our kinaesthetic sense. In each case our senses are used for a "non-utilitarian" pursuit and in educating them we aim at the same time at educating appreciation of the art form. The problem is, however, how to stimulate sensory reactions and to develop the capacity to differentiate an increasing variety of finer shades of sensations, or even of any sensation at all. Anyone who has lost the function of a sense organ will not be able to refine its capacity; there is none there to be refined. The fact that other senses tend to compensate for the lack shows that the sensations received are the result of a combination of different sense impressions. This speaks for the importance of education through dance, as here the kinaesthetic sense, which is central, together with the contribution from all the other senses, has a chance of opening the door to awareness of self in a social and objective environment. This will, however, not be possible without a conscious process and an intellectual understanding of the elements involved.

In an attempt to educate our movement sense we might elicit from our personal style of moving traits which have universal validity and represent therefore basic material for learning. Conversely, we might familiarise ourselves directly with fundamental movement processes by practising selected movement units and assimilating their distinctive nature. Laban has exposed the elements of which movement is compounded and has presented in this book many essential facts about human movement which are of invaluable help in a learning process. It must, however, be remembered that knowledge of these is meant only to stimulate and to elicit responses from the whole being in an all-round and varied way.

There are also fundamental conditions influencing the movements of the body which have to be taken into consideration. Let us, therefore, look at those which are particularly relevant here.

Fundamental conditions influencing bodily movement

As already mentioned, the body is the instrument with which the various forms of the art of movement are produced. Unlike the instruments which we fashion for use in the other arts, and which are fundamentally extensions and specialised developments of the human body and its functions, the instrument used in the art of movement is given to us. The problem is only how to make the best use of it and how to develop its functions. We do not have to invent the instrument itself.

For the purpose of establishing a basis for training and body discipline, it will be useful to review some of the natural functions of the human body and of the physiological and psychological processes which govern them. The following considerations are relevant here:

—The alternating tension (pull) and relaxation present in all neuromuscular actions.

—The expansion and contraction of the thorax in breathing.

—The dynamic character of the balance required in upright posture.

—The counter-movement of arms and legs in locomotion.

—The pendular swings of the extremities in shoulder and hip joints.

—The springiness in knee and ankle joints.

—The bending, twisting, turning, and undulating actions of the arms through a series of joints—that of shoulders, elbows, wrists, and fingers.

—The lifting action against the force of gravity and the dropping of the body by its own weight.

—The nervous equilibrium in all physiological functions (natural economy of the human organism's energy).

—The mark of mental features and qualities of personality on movement functions.

—The influence of environment and events on the movements of the body.

—The possibility of forming a great variety of new movement patterns; man's ability to adapt and learn.

Material

The material of the art of movement is the physical properties of the movements of the human body, which we shape and mould like a potter his clay, giving it intensity, rhythm, stress, coherence in form, in short, vital expression of the experience of life. This requires craftsmanship and knowledge (in the body) of the essential nature of the material and how to handle it.

The natural accidents of weight, time, space, flow, which activate motion, play here an important role. Laban called them "motion factors" and showed how the human being with his mental and physical capacities can relate to them. In fact, as long as we are alive we are compelled to deal with these factors, since this lies in the nature of our existence. So we are spending an energy, consciously or unconsciously, fundamentally to sustain life and ultimately to enjoy it and fulfil the purpose we see in it. Laban referred to this energy as "effort" which springs from inner impulses, desires, intentions, moods, and drives, and which manifests itself in the movements of our body. In Chapter IV he gives a systematic survey of rudimentary effort experiments, which will be helpful in the building up of what he called a free dance technique. They mainly refer to the actions in relation to weight, space, and time and occasionally allow the experience of the different qualities in the flow of movement to develop naturally from them.

In order to acquire craftsmanship in dance we need to master:

—our muscular energy, or force, as needed to resist gravitation, including intensification and the opposite;

—the speed of our actions within the passage of time, including acceleration and the opposite;

—the extension of our movements along determined spatial pathways, including multiplicity of directions and the opposite;

—the various possibilities of their combination, as well as the fluency and continuity of movement forms, including their stabilisation and the pauses arising.

When growing up, we acquire a certain mastery of such combinations as a matter of course, and along with some specific skills which we need in everyday living, we develop certain habitual ways of performing them. Dance as a means of education provides varied challenges for a person's effort responses which in the context of a dance situation are directed towards the creation of a meaningful whole. The mental, physical, and emotional components of the dance movement need to appear in distinct actions of the body and through them in significant shapes in space. Failing this, no dance will come into being, which could have given the dancer a stimulating experience, an opportunity to enhance his sensitivity and enrich his responses. A dance technique must be directed towards such an aim. Therefore the exercises will not only need to be rhythmic, dynamic, and clear in shape but they must also be executed with an inner awareness of the whole movement form. This in turn will affect what Laban called the "thinking in terms of movement" which can be stimulated to find variations, developments, contrasts, as well as new transitions and links. Thus a person's movement vocabulary gets gradually developed and consists of fundamental and universal movement occurrences.

When we have acquired a certain basic vocabulary and are beginning to think in terms of movement we can then improve the mastery of the performance of movement units or sequences of them. Technical development in educational dance goes hand in hand with a comprehension of the movement content. This is a slow process with many stages of maturation, but at every stage a unity of acting, thinking, and feeling should be achieved.

Technique

Every kind of dance technique contains rudiments of movement. Which of these are stressed and cultivated depends on the type of dance it serves, as a technique is always directed towards acquiring the special expertness of execution needed in a particular style.

Most dance techniques which have been developed are usually bound to a more or less limited and concise selection of fundamental exercises for bodily mastery. This makes it possible to reach a very high degree of skill in the particular mode of moving. Many a time, however, the sharpening of the tool and the conditioning of the instrument assume such importance that the exploration of the movement material is neglected, and the vocabulary acquired is only sparse.

In educational dance, with its aim to help a person to realise and enhance his own potential, to learn to relate and to increase responsiveness and ability to communicate, the technical equipment has in the first place to serve that end. This is why Laban advocated a "free" dance technique, one that is free from a particularly fashioned style, but by no means chaotically free. There are the universal rhythm and form elements which are part of our human make-up and experience. These we try to touch and elicit from within ourselves, and in bringing them up into consciousness our creative powers may be enriched. We need to steep ourselves with our whole being in the material of movement and to discover what facility or difficulty we have in using and treating it when dancing. This will give us a greater understanding of ourselves and stimulate us to develop our potential.

Styles

At the same time it is most rewarding to acquaint oneself with different dance styles and even learn to master one or two. There are historical styles and ethnic ones, some serving social functions, others religious worship and ritual. Many stem from groups of people, others have been created by individual artists and dancing masters. A few have acquired classical status, while others are in the popular domain.

Another interesting study is to find out what the particular features of a style are. In order to determine this, a simple guideline, such as the following, may be of practical assistance: how is the body used in space and with what kind of effort? Although this may at first sight appear not always to have a direct bearing on what one sees, does, or feels, the complex of the basic subdivisions of each aspect provides for a multitude of combinations out of which only a few are typical for a particular style of dance expression.

It will be quickly recognised that the main questions concern the carriage of the body, the placing of feet and their relation to the floor, the kind of control in the shaping of gestures and positions, characteristic time patterns and placement of accents, the parts of the body in which the movement is activated and carried out, and the typical sequences of effort stresses.

Rhythm

The art of movement, and particularly dance, is dependent on one uniform principle, that of rhythmic unity. The intrinsic quality of rhythm is periodic repetition, and each periodic, or rhythmic, event shows aspects of both structural configuration and kinetic–dynamic flux. The body with its various parts modifies the nature of the rhythmic pattern depending on how it is used in producing the movement. When we create a movement sequence we do two things, consciously or unconsciously: we search for a satisfying spatial composition in which our inner impulses, or efforts, can find an appropriate visible form; and we try to feel into the shapes, with which the movements of our limbs and body fill the space around us, and to respond to them from within. These two procedures are not necessarily a matter of succession of one and then the other; on the contrary, a simultaneous awareness of the inward- and outward-going flow heightens the feel-

ing of "being in one's body"and then it seems to us
that we really dance. The distinctive qualities of the
rhythms in dance movement will depend on the particular relationship of effort and shape, and this is
manifested in the body.

The body can be set into motion through an oscillation or a pendulum-like swing. For instance, when
swinging our body to and fro elastically from one leg
on to the other and then giving it a special impetus—
as if throwing a parcel—it is transported to another
spot. This may be rhythmically repeated several times
until we can respond to the sensation and begin to enjoy the experience. Together with the enjoyment, an
increasing feeling of vitality is likely to arise and a
desire to select definite places in the room at which to
arrive with each swing. Much as we are induced,
when singing a couple of particular notes, to add
several others to them and to make up a melody, so,
through clearly defining a goal for each swing and thus
enhancing liveliness, we are motivated to continue the
movement experience and to make up a movement
sequence.

In this way new responses are stimulated and movement imagination is enriched. Through repetition a
memory is built up, providing a storehouse of experience, which in turn is necessary for new inspirations to
arise, sensitivity to grow, and a greater understanding
to develop. As soon as we can get wholly involved in
the movement happening and respond to it with our
human nature our inventive resources are likely to
open up, creating shapes and rhythms with an increasingly greater richness and clarity. The unified form
of the movement is an expression of inner values, and

since it serves no utilitarian purpose, we consider it to be an artistic expression.

The rhythms of the bodily actions with their effort and spatial components may be monotonous or variable "conformant" or "disformant," but whatever they are, they must be imbued with life. Our emotional responses, our will to act, our dreams and aspirations, in short the whole gamut of our inner world needs to be stirred and brought into harmonious relationship with the form-giving elements without.

In movement, through rhythms embracing increases and decreases, inner participation is heightened and awareness of change stimulated. This can range from the height of excitement to the utmost calmness and stillness and include the various moods which express themselves in the mixtures of the two.

Increases and decreases should be experienced of:

speed ⎫ each as a single factor in the
intensity ⎪ rhythmic wave of a movement, as
size ⎬ well as in combinations of two,
fluency ⎭ three, or all four components.

This can become quite exciting, particularly when cross-combinations are made, such as, for instance, an increase of speed and size (length of step) in stepping, coupled with a decrease of intensity (muscular tension) and fluency (continuity) leading to a staccato-like onward movement with weakening legs as they reach further and further out in quickening succession. In a circulating arm gesture, when an increase of size and fluency is coupled with a decrease of intensity while keeping a steady speed or tempo, a feeling of undisturbed continuity is gradually created by the successive rounds of the growing spiral.

The body in space

Let us now consider ourselves, that is our corporal presence in space. The characteristic quality of space is extension, and as was said in Chapter V "wherever the body moves or stands, it is surrounded by space" and "all movement takes place by transferring the body or parts of the body from one position in space to another." This latter remark refers, of course, to those movements in which the centre of the whole body, or of the moving parts of the body, is shifted and progresses through space. The central area of the body seeks another situation in space, and in all forms of locomotion, such as stepping, jumping, leaping, rolling, etc., the centre of gravity is transported to a new location. It may be thrown up or dropped down, or carried from spot to spot as previously described in the movement sequence developed from the oscillation of the body.

Small parts of the body, with their own central areas, can also travel distances through space, but these may be only very short. When gesturing with an arm the limb moves from one place to another; when bowing, the centre of levity, the sternum, carries shoulders and head through space downward; the lips protrude forward when pouting in disappointment, or withdraw backward in fear; brows and jaw jut out in anger and an ear turns the head in listening.

But there is yet another aspect of bodily movement in space, that of expanding and contracting. This refers to an awareness that "wherever the body moves or stands, it is surrounded by space." It is a spreading out from a centre either of the whole body, or a part of it, into any direction around. The centre itself is not transported to another location, and therefore no particular pathway or line of progression through space becomes evident. They are minute extensions, and, of course, also contractions, within the body which give a feeling of growing and shrinking, of waxing and waning, and, with it, a streaming forth into a multitude of directions without and a binding together in one centre within. It is, so to speak, the life of space, its "breathing", and it is in fact closely connected with the physiological function of respiration. A conscious awareness and control of expansion and contraction of the thorax in respiration will help in the experience of our body being in space.

When influenced by a growing or shrinking tendency in the central area, our arms and legs are enlivened as they strive away from or towards the body centre, but without travelling through space. The movement flow reaches the upper extremities via the shoulder girdle, and the lower ones via the pelvic girdle. In small areas of the body a similar experience can be gained, for example, of fingers around the centre of the palm, or the mouth around its centre between the lips, or the eyelids around the centres of the eyeballs.

The movements of spreading and traversing are two fundamental spatial actions, which relate us in two different ways to the world without, and their interplay can be both in sequence and simultaneous. In spreading, we considered the movements outward and inward, growing and shrinking, expanding and contracting. Now let us look once more at those of traversing. When we shift our body, or a part of it, to a new place we are progressing through space, but when, after several shifts, we return to the point of departure we are circling in space. Progressing and circling have entirely different functions in dance expression, which is an interesting area to explore. For instance:

(*a*) The body is in a broad bent-down position with first a shrinking and then an expanding tendency throughout; after the body has been erected and the feet pulled together an arm performs a large circling gesture.

(*b*) A progressing stepping motion is followed by a contracting and shrinking tendency in the pelvic girdle and legs, *i.e.* a pulling or shrivelling inward of the surfaces towards the bones as if feeling cold.

The actions in each of these two examples may also happen simultaneously:

(*c*) An arm performs a circling gesture while shrinking and expanding (in the feel of its own volume and not by bending or stretching).

(*d*) Stepping onward while shrinking, but without appreciably dropping the pelvic girdle or bending the legs.

Of course, many other combinations and cross-combinations can be made and composed into longer sequences, involving in the actions different parts of the body, and different directions and locations in space.

In addition, we may bring in some of the other factors contributing to the rhythmic form of a movement event, which we discussed earlier on, namely those of increasing and decreasing speed, intensity, size, and fluency. A systematic exploration of the influences of the various movement elements upon one another, both simultaneous and in sequence, is essential in dance education. The imagination needs a store of specific movement experiences from which to draw, mostly unconsciously, when creating a sequence of dance, mime, or drama, in fact any expressive utterance produced by bodily activity, including speaking and singing.

Dynamics of spatial tensions

It now remains to consider the shape and dynamic quality of the pathways which the body produces when traversing space and the flow character of its expanding and contracting actions.

Intellectually it is easy to grasp that three main directional extensions can describe the three-dimensional nature of space; in the body we can experience them by first of all deliberately erecting ourselves in the natural upright stance and spreading our arms out sideways. These two extensions are inherent in our body structure and stressed in our carriage. The pull by the nape of the neck and head through the centre line of the body away from the ground, with the feet firmly anchored, gives a clear feel of the dimension of height. The body is delicately poised in this anti-gravitational position, and together with the feeling of breadth, brought about by its bilateral structure and the sideways spreading of the torso, which balances the shoulder girdle, a flat cross of the dimensions of height and breadth is produced. This represents the standard by which we assess the directions and locations of our movements.

We experience the third extension through the actions of our limbs in the locomotion of our legs forward and backward and in the gathering and scattering actions of our arms. It is the time factor which has entered here, adding the experience of traversing space to that of spreading and filling it. The three-dimensional cross can therefore be seen to relate to the motion factors of weight in the up–down dimension, of space in the spreading of the side–side dimension, and of time in the activities producing the forward–backward dimension.

The dancer, consciously or unconsciously, tends to bring the carriage of his body into line with one or more of these three dimensions when he controls and restrains progression, or change in the combinations of movement, or when bringing it to a termination. They are the vertical and horizontal tensions of the body in space, with their completely symmetric balance, which have a stabilising effect.

In contrast, the body quickly appreciates the liberation when its movements are deflected from the comparatively balanced condition within the dimensional system. When we are roused our body balance becomes more labile, we enter a state of greater readiness for change and the symmetric countenance is given up for an asymmetric one. Flow of movement is enhanced, which has to continue until the onward-flowing excitement recedes and is finally calmly contained.

Utmost liberation is experienced when our movements are directed towards a diagonal (*see* Chapter V, p. 86). We can convince ourselves of this by making the following experiment. Let us stand with both feet closely together—it does not matter whether in a paral-

lel position or with an outward rotation of the legs—
and introduce a spreading movement from the central
area of the body towards high–right–forward. We
shall find ourselves in a rather labile situation, from
which progression through space is easily forthcoming,
or even required. Our weight is not only shifted on
to the right foot but also raised on to the ball of it, towards the outer edge, and thus perched as if ready to
fly. Now we shall use this initial preparation and follow
it up with a clear intention of traversing space. By
taking a step diagonally forward away from the stance,
and at the same time tossing our weight upward
towards the direction high–right–forward, a kind of
flying jump will result. For a brief moment we shall
find ourselves freely flowing through space and experiencing a sense of unshackled release. There is,
however, a certain amount of daring and courage involved as our system does not like to lose the security
of an equilibrated situation. A similar experience can
be gained when the central body area expands and
moves towards any of the other diagonal directions.
Moving to the lower ones, however, leads ultimately to
falling and cessation of movement. As we were able to
relate the dimensional cross to the motion factors of
weight, space, and time, it can now be appreciated that
the diagonal cross relates to the motion factor of flow.

Movement arises out of stillness and recedes into
stillness. Thus there are two opposing tendencies,
one which initiates movement and keeps it going and
the other which induces it to fade away and terminate.
The excitement we feel, which makes us want to continue the movement experience, causes us to delay a
return to stability, in which gravitation asserts itself,

and to dwell on the labile state of equilibrium which demands continuous adaptation to change.

The stable and labile qualities of movement are fundamental aspects of space. The motion factor of flow, as expounded by Laban, is based on the concept of freeing and binding. Movement events in dance unfold from the interplay of these freeing and binding forces, as well as the alternating states of lability and stability. The ultimate of each of these latter states is achieved only at outstanding moments, those of highest excitement and of complete repose. Most dance movements are influenced by both states simultaneously and fluctuate between them.

It is a rewarding study to invent and perform movement sequences to help us become aware of this fluctuation. They should embrace moments of greatest change in the central area of the body, as well as periods when it is carefully controlled and in line with the gravitational pull. This can lead to a theme for a dance in which the dancer's personal imaginative responses and intentions produce the moods or the drama of its content. ,

Trace-forms of movement

Shape in movement is created by a series of directional tendencies which are followed by a part of the body or the whole of it. The body is a three-dimensional figure with many articulations, and the shape of a movement is never just the circumference of a flat pattern, but has a plastic character. The actual form which a dance gesture takes depends on the kind of effort rhythm with which it is produced and how the various body articulations are involved in it. In his book *Choreutics* (pp. 46–47) Laban demonstrates that the simple raising of an arm traces "a form resembling the shape of an opening fan"; when the hand follows smoothly and steadily the configuration of a circle with an extended arm gesture, a cone-shaped trace-form is created.

Most of the time we are only aware of the outline shape which we trace with our arms and legs in the kinesphere or on the floor and, indeed, we select particular basic configurations in order to train our kin-aesthetic sense and appreciation of form. Beyond this "a trace-form supplies a certain inspiration as does a melody; the details of the execution of it by the body can often be left to the individual taste of the performer". (See *Choreutics*, p. 49.)

In order to experience a labile state of the body within a particular trace-form, and as we have seen, this demands continuity of movement, we shall take as an example a circuit pathway through our kinesphere and around our body. Each directional indication given must in this case be initiated by the central area of the body, sending the directional flux of the movement towards the extremities. In this way, not only the whole trunk is involved in the bending, raising, and twisting actions but also the legs, which produce shifts of weight in stepping along a circular floor pattern, while the arms are tracing a wave-like circuit in the air. Here is the circuit: *hlb—dlf—hrf—drb—hlb* (for meaning of abbreviations see Fig. 2).

It will be noticed that this circuit is formed by diagonal directions, but, in aiming at bringing out the circling character of this trace-form, the movement towards each direction needs to be somewhat curtailed.

Each time as the directional goal is nearly reached the next one is already anticipated, thus rounding and smoothing the transitions. There is also a dropping and rising in the circuit which promotes acceleration and deceleration together with an alternation of more or less intensity of stress. These increases and decreases in size, speed, and intensity within the fluent continuation of a circling and undulating pathway tend to create a mood of animated tranquillity and harmony.

In contrast let us try the following configuration which progresses through the kinesphere. Although it is to be executed symmetrically, each of the single sections of which the trace-form is composed pulls the body out of its normal comparatively stable situation. The central area is again strongly involved in the movement, and the accompanying steps enhance the dynamic content of the sequence. This time we are using directional aims which lie half-way between the diagonals; they are called diametrical directions (see Chap. V, p. 86). First of all we have to ascertain our stance and then step a small distance backward on to the right foot as our arms cross, with each hand reaching past the opposite hip, and the small of the back pulling backward. We are now ready to start the sequence of progression through our kinesphere thus:

right arm:	*lb*	—	*hr*	—	*fd*	—	*rb*
left arm:	*rb*	—	*hl*	—	*fd*	—	*lb*
steps	right:	*b*	—return to			—	*b*
	left:		original				
			stance on	—	*ɟ*		
			both feet				
			high				

This sequence develops a progression from a very narrow and slightly concaved position to a very wide one convexed in the trunk. The stages of development pass through broadening of the chest, with erecting of spine and raising of arms, to a lunging and dipping forward an appreciable distance. The side-side orientation is at this point eliminated, and the hands join together, as the face and eyes look at them. This produces a tractive force forward–downward which gives a dynamic preparation for a backward release in which the trunk arches and the arms and hands separate, each to its own side of the body, slightly dropping down from the shoulders. The chest and the face are turned forward–upward, giving the end position a radiant, open, and strong expression.

Gestures of the limbs, circling or progressing through the kinesphere, travel away from, towards, or around the body. It is in the nature of the sphere and the structure of the body that smooth continuation of the movement flow is achieved through curving the pathways, particularly when the limit has been reached, either at the periphery of the sphere or at the centre of it. In this way curved, rounded, or wavelike traces are created, as illustrated in the earlier example of the undulating circular pathway.

The latter example, in which the movement progresses onward through the kinesphere, introduces a new idea. The gestures producing the trace-form go through three stages before completing it, and are fully extended each time to the periphery of the sphere. Without curving the pathways, we approach the next goal in a more or less direct manner, which involves the arms in a definite bending and stretching activity. The trace-form has sharp edges and decisive points where the new directional pull is introduced. The concaving and convexing of the spine and the trunk complete the inner structure of the trace-form with complementary curves, thus creating an organic progression through the kinesphere. The trace-form has, however, a sharp, accented, and dynamic character.

Lastly, let us look at gestures which are initiated by the part or parts of the moving limb farthest away from the body centre, which should now remain contained and provide a steady counterpole to the gestures. Awareness of the arising trace-form is in this case mainly of the configuration of its outline. The movements tend to have either very sudden and sharp directional changes or are measured, without an increasing or decreasing intensity and speed. The outline may be curved, angular, or undulating; it may be drawn near the body or far from it, or travel from near to far. Whatever trace it makes, the gesture has as its antagonist the central area of the body which establishes a specific posture as a counter to it. This gives the movement expression a certain feeling of detachment, aloofness, and constrained power.

We have considered three examples of trace-forms:

(a) The circling, undulating track, produced by a confluency of torso movements, arm gestures, and accompanying steps.

(b) The progressing track from a narrow to a wide position in which the torso movements, arm gestures, and steps complement one another.

(c) The track created by the extremities, with the

central body area assuming a definite posture as a counter-pole.

We can see how their structures are built up by the interplay of the whole body. These consist of tensions between points and planes; and the relationship between the single parts of a trace-form produces dynamic and plastic activity. The quality of this is influenced by the kind of effort with which we perform the concurrent or crossing lines and planes, pull them into different directions, and concentrate them, or set them a distance apart. Creating, transforming, and dissolving trace-forms, this is the play we pursue when dancing. As effort impulses and images of our mind materialise in the movements of our body, trace-forms are spontaneously or deliberately created. It is, however, useful to study the types of fundamental relationships between lines and planes as Laban introduced them in Chapter V. In order to grasp their significance we must endeavour to make such trace-forms, which are presented to us from without, our own by responding with movement, imagination, and enjoyment and giving them personal bodily expression.

Sometimes, however, we find that gestures follow incongruous tracks, and postures change in a disconnected way, so that they do not combine into a coherent whole. Such isolated utterances can be very eloquent and give the dancer a chance to experience the manifestation of a single effort expression. This will be highlighted if the gesture is clearly related spatially not only to the central area of the body and its particular carriage but also to other parts of the body, which may be still or moving, and to the floor.

Distinct spatial movement statements will arise such as: away from, towards, parallel with, above, below, crossing, approaching, diverging, meeting, aside, around, near, far, together, and many more. The dancer must aim at getting a clear feel of the kinds of relation which the parts of the body have to one another, to the floor, as well as to the kinesphere.

Conclusion

The sixteen basic movement themes in Chapter III contain several sections on movement in space. There Laban gives a systematic introduction to this problem. As he used to say, one can write down only facts; everything else is poetry. But the fact of a definite trace-form or circuit in space is more than a mere outline of a design; it contains its own particular shapes, tractive forces, and tensions.

As already pointed out, trace-forms provide a challenge for the dancer. On the one hand, through feeling into them, he brings out their inherent kinetic qualities according to his own vision and inner resources of energy, thus giving them poetic or dramatic life. On the other, he has to find and create forms which are suitable to express his dance idea, as significant form is the instrument of vital expression.

Movement is basic to life. It is there in all of us, but to make use of its power we need to become aware of it, and learn to recognise its principles and experience its forms. Our efforts engender form, and form engenders effort. The body, with its various parts, can function like an orchestra; the single parts may follow one another in producing a complete movement form, or they may combine in concerted action, (see p. 38, Theme 12).

They may be confluent or divergent, some taking the lead, while others are accompanying or producing a still counter-pole. The dance intention directs the various actions, and in the realisation the entire being is drawn into a unified whole.

A cultivated sensibility for movement and a heightened perception of it are a necessary part of our capacity to relate to the world and to each other. In dancing we are able to experience relationships in which awareness of self and others is enhanced. The feeling of joy which dance can give helps us to harmonise ourselves and to gain an increased sense of belonging. For this our inherent movement impulse needs to be vitalised and guided towards a full and structured expression. When we are sufficiently moved and achieve genuine expression in dance, then we begin to dismantle the barriers which have been built by our manner of living and the mental atmosphere in which we grow up. If in our teaching we have helped people to tackle their fears and gain confidence to communicate freely, sensitively, and imaginatively; if we have enabled them to become, even to a small extent, aware of their own potential and that of others, then we will have achieved a good measure of success. Such success is the justification of education through dance.

INDEX

A

Academic studies, 32, 100
Accents, 95
Action(s), balanced use of, 52
  basic effort, 34–36, 53, 56, 102
  bodily, 98
  chains and sequences of, 106
  combination of, 80
  dancing, 41
  incomplete, 96
  isolated, 31, 32
  language of, 44
  moods, 44, 45, 46
  natural, 14
  rhythmic, 17
  single, 82
Activities, physical, 100, 105
Activity, dynamic and plastic, 132
  primary of man, 15
Adolescents, 50
Age-groups, 33, 50
Angle, 89
Art education, 29, 104
Art of movement, 2, 3, 7, 8, 9, 110, 112, 113
  material of, 114, 118
Artifact, 109
Automatised, 37

B

Balance, 125
Ballet d'Action, 3, 4
Behaviour, traits of, 99
Body, and mind, 44
  awareness of, 29

circumvention of, 88
discipline, 113
instrumental use of, 31, 108, 112
isolated parts of, 101
parts of, 30, 40, 59, 61, 63, 65, 67, 69, 72, 74, 121, 133
Bound, 46, 56
Boundness, controlled, 74
Bowling, 80
Breaking, 83

C

Carried, 98
Central, 36
Centre, body, 14, 93
  of gravity, 121
  of sphere, 86, 87, 88, 91
Change, harmonious (of effort), 102
Child, effect of dance on, 105
  watching a, 102
Children, bodily and mental food for, 105
  development of personality, 43
Child's bodily and mental attitude, 107
Circuits, 89, 90, 91, 133
Class, attitude of, 99
  behind desks, 100
  dull, 99
  excitable, 99
  spirit of, 99
Clearness and perfection, degrees of, 44

Communication between people, 97, 98
Compressing of resilient objects, 75
Counter-direction, 86, 87
Counter-tension, elastic, 60, 62, 64, 66, 68, 70, 73, 74, 75
Creative ability, 11, 12, 13, 29, 51, 117
Cube, 86, 87, 88, 90
Cube-octahedron, 90, 91

D

Dab, 34
Dabbing, 22, 69–71, 75, 83
Dance, 108, 110, 115
  Central European, v
  composition, 11, 50, 51
  craftmanship in, 114, 115
  dramatic, 5
  educational value of, 104–106
  expression, 3, 5, 98
  forms, 106
    social, 9, 10
    stylised, 10
  fundamental art of man, 2, 7
  language of, 109
  lyricism, 5, 50
  material of, 109
  modern, v, 3, 7, 10, 11, 27
  social life and, 2
  social value of, 98
  styles, 96
  teacher, tastes of the, 49
  technique, 115, 116, 117
  theatrical, 9
  tradition of, 2
  traditional and modern, differences between, 10
  traditional technique, 9
  training, 8, 20, 21, 23, 24, 25
  urge to, 17, 18, 19, 105
Dancer, professional, 110

Dances, communal, 12
  historical, 96
  individual, 104
  primitive, 14
Dancing, 134
  creative activity of, 109
  pleasure given by, 106
Danse libre, v
Derivatives of basic actions, 82
Development, lop-sided, 48
Direct, 15, 46, 70
Diagonals, 87, 88, 125, 126
Diameters, 87, 88
Dimensions, 86, 88, 125
Dragging, 83
Dramatic expression, 48
Dramatics, 24
Drums, 95
Duncan, Isadora, 5, 6
Dynamic(s), 124, 132
  content, 129

E

Education, 109
  through dance, 112, 134
Educational dance, 116, 117
Educational task, 99
Effort(s), 8, 18, 19, 20, 21, 26, 54, 108, 114
  akin, 34, 35
  and relaxation, 52
  attitudes, discordant, 106
  balance, disturbed, 104
  balance of, 19, 53, 100, 101
  bodily and mental, 44, 102
  contrast(ing), 34, 35, 102
  control, 16, 60, 62, 64, 66, 68, 70, 72, 75, 96
  deficiencies, 106
  elements, 8, 46
  experience, 132
  expression, 53
  gamut of, 23

instinctive, 14
intellectual, 24
life, 49, 105, 106
mutations or changes of, 47
rhythm, 75–79
sign of, 55
study, 15, 80, 100, 101
training, 24
transitions, 32, 34, 80, 96, 102
Elevation from ground, 41
Emotion(s), 102
language of, 44
Energy, economy of, 53
living, 101
Exertion, bodily and mental, 101
Explosions, 64

F

Falling, 71, 83
Firm, 46
Flapping, 83
Flexible, 15, 46, 68
Flick, 34
Flicking, 19, 60–62, 73, 83
derivatives of, 83
Flipping, 81
Float, 34
Floating, 19
or flying, 65–66, 73
Floor pattern, 22
Flow, 8, 22, 56, 57, 58, 114, 126, 127, 130
absence of, 102
awareness of, 30
concept of freeing and binding, 127
free or bound, 56, 57
Fluency, decreased, 71
freedom of, 72
or boundness, combinations of, 57
Fluttering movement, 62

Frustrations, removal of, 19
Fumbling, 83

G

Games, 24, 100, 105
Gestures, 130, 131, 132
Glide, 34
Gliding, 71, 73–75, 83
Graphs, 54
Grasping and gathering, 16
Groping, 83
Group dances, 104
feeling, 42
formations, 43
Growing, 42, 83
Gymnastics, 24, 100
teacher of, 103

H

Harmony and melody, 95
personal and social, 105
Hovering, of a feather, 62
Human relationship, 104
Hurrying, 83

I

Imagery, 110
Immobility, ideal of, 19
Impulse, 26, 27
Impulses, mental, 18
Industrial civilisation, 54
Inspiration, musical, dramatic, 57
Integrate, intellectual knowledge with creative ability, 13
Intellectual form of expression, 52

J

Jerking, 65, 83
Joints, co-ordination of, 18
Jumping in the air, 58

Jumps, 41, 92
  turning, 72, 93

K

Kicking, 15, 16, 17, 83
Kicks, 41
Kinaesthetic sense, 111, 112, 128
Kinesphere, 91, 92
Knowledge, of our days, 106

L

Labile, 125, 126, 127, 128
Leaps, 41
  turning, 42
Light, 46
  or fine touch, 62
Line, 89
Locomotion, 31

M

Management, scientific, 4
  activity, 104
Mental and bodily state, discord
  in, 102
Mind, 102
  activity of, 25
  and body, 22
Mobility, degrees of, 92
Mood, apathetic, 101
Motion factors, 22, 24, 114, 125,
  126, 127
Motor sensations, 111
Movement, 109, 126, 133
  awareness, 110
  basic forms of, 109
  dance-like, repetitive, 20
  drama, 50
  eddies and waves of, 51
  educational value of, 5, 9, 97,
  106
  elements of, 34, 44

essence of life, 101
expression, 3, 4, 10, 45, 46
flow of, 6, 10, 11–13, 20, 30, 47,
  96, 97, 98, 110, 125
habits, 3, 6, 25, 103
ideas, 28
imagination, 119, 132
in space, 94
interpretation, 99
language of, 26
mechanical performance of, 106
memory, 31, 33, 42, 119
moods of, 46–48
narrow, 30, 93
observation, 21, 23, 42, 97, 106
of everyday life, 25
phrases of, 44
poetry of, 6
psycho-physical experience of,
  111
research, industrial, 4, 6, 8, 11
sense of, 110, 111, 112
sequence(s), 118, 119, 137
shapes and rhythms of, 45, 47
significance of, 103
sphere of, 85
spirit of, in education, 10
statements, 133
studies, 29
swinging, 54
training, in factories and schools,
  11
vocabulary, 109, 116
wide, 30, 93
Movements, deficient, 13
  grotesque, 40
  hesitating, 100
  large or small, 84
Mover, mental state of, 102
Moving, technique of, 9
Muscle actions, smallest, 84, 99
  groups, antagonistic, 60
Muscles, antagonistic, 75
  of face, 84

Music, 95
  interpretation, 93
  set, 51

N

Noises, making, 17
Noverre, Jean George, 3, 4

O

Octahedron, 90
Operations, industrial, 10
Opinions, 99
Orientation points, 88
Over-correction, 21

P

Painting, 101
Participation, inner, 57
Partners, adaptation to, 30
Path(ways), 27, 85, 88, 91, 92, 94
Patterns in space, 33, 37, 43, 89
Patting, 83
Penetrating, 83
People, adaptation to one another, 104
  assessing, 99
  unbalanced, 100
Percussion instruments, 95
Personal and social harmony, 105
  characteristics, 47
  experience (of effort), 105
Personality, 12
  development of child's, 44
  growth of, 106
  traits of, 99
Physical exercise, 105
Piercing, 83
Play-forms, 28
Plucking, 83
Poking, 83

Position(s) in the trunk, 130
Posture, 131, 132
Preparation, 75
Press, 34
Pressing, 19, 22, 59, 60, 75, 82
Pressure of weight, 62
Pulling, 83
Punch, 15, 34, 63–65, 83

Q

Quadrangle, 89
Quick, 16, 64

R

Reactions of groups, 81–82
Recreation, 109
Relaxation, 53–54
Rest, 53
Rhythm, 17, 32, 75, 94, 118, 120
  and shapes, 54, 94, 96, 98, 119
  audible, 95
  concentration on, 98
  effort, 75–79
  embracing increases and decreases, 120, 129
  in dance movement, 119
  musical, 95
  prosodic notation of, 95
Rhythmic form, 123
Rhythms, occupational, 32
  of sounds, 95
Rising, 83
Row and circle, 43

S

Scale, 27
Self-consciousness, 21
  development, 14
  training, 14
Sensory reactions, 111
Shaking, 70, 83

Shape(s), 27, 36, 37, 38, 91, 94, 108, 127
Shooting, 71
Shoving, 83
Shrinking, 42, 83
Singing, 51, 97, 101
Skill, bodily, 101, 104
Slash, 34
Slashing, 15, 65, 71–73
  derivatives of, 83
Smearing, 83
Smoothing, 83
Smudging, 83
Somersaults, 38
Space, 8, 22, 27, 60, 62, 108, 114, 125, 126
  awareness of, 30
  body in, 121, 124
  circling in, 123, 130, 131
  expanding and contracting in, 121, 124
  general, 85
  orientation in, 36, 86
  personal, 85
  progressing through, 121, 123, 125, 126, 130, 131
  quality, 96
  stretches of, 94
Spatial tensions, 124
Speaking, 97, 101
Spine, flexibility of, 38
Spirit of the past, 106
Spontaneity, the child's, 21
Spontaneous faculty of man, 11, 12
Sport, 80, 109
Spreading and traversing, 122, 123, 126
Stability, 125, 126, 127
Stance, 85, 86
Stiffening, 83
Stirring, 83
Streaming, 71
Stretching, 83

Strewing, 83
Stroking, 83
Style(s), 117, 118
Success, intellectual, 104
Sudden, 46, 64
Sustained, 16, 46, 66

T

Tapping, 83
Taste, artistic, 51
Taylor, Frederick, W., 4, 5
Technique, of moving, 9
  dance, 9, 10, 11, 13
Tennis, serving in, 80
Tensions, detrimental inner, 97
Termination, 75
Throwing, 83
Thrusting, 15, 19, 22, 63–65, 73, 75, 83
Time, 8, 22, 60, 82, 114, 125, 126
  quality, 96
  rhythm, 94
  stretch of, 94
Trace-form(s) of movement, 127–133
Training, basis for, 113
  teacher's, 103
Transitions, harmonious, 102
Triangle, 89
Turn, 93

V

Variations of leg gestures, 95
  of movement themes, 28
Vibrating, 70
Vitality, 119

W

Water, whirls and eddies of, 68
Weight, 8, 22, 30, 60, 62, 114, 125, 126

Well-being, individual and collective, 53
Whipping, 83
Whirls and eddies, 68
Whisking, 79
Width, 23
Work, 109
Working actions, 3, 11, 25, 32
    efficiency, 8

habits, 6
Wring, 34
Wringing, 15, 63, 67–69, 75, 83
    out a cloth, 67
Writing, 97, 101

Z

Zones of limbs, 27, 92

More Books on
Educational Movement & Dance

Choreutics
RUDOLF LABAN
Annotated and edited by
LISA ULLMANN

This important, large-format work deals exhaustively with the analysis and synthesis of movement. The text gives a comprehensive survey of the principles underlying Laban's concepts of space harmony, and many examples are included. Special reproduction techniques have preserved the spirit of many of Laban's original drawings, and the use of colour adds to the value of the illustrations.

Illustrated

Creative Dance in the Primary School
JOAN RUSSELL

This large-format book explains in great practical detail, with the aid of photographs, how Laban's ideas can be put to work in the primary school. Ways of presenting dance to children are discussed, and the basic theory is analysed and then applied in a specimen planned lesson which has been used by a number of local education authorities. For the latest edition a new chapter entitled "The Role of the Teacher" has been added and new photographs included.

Illustrated

Creative Dance in the Secondary School
JOAN RUSSELL

This companion volume to *Creative Dance in the Primary School* presents the case for including the art of movement in the middle and secondary school curriculum. It stresses the need for creative activity to balance the academic work. For the latest edition, the text has been fully revised and updated.

Illustrated

Dictionary of Kinetography Laban
ALBRECHT KNUST

This large-format book is primarily a reference book, in which kinetographers — those who use Rudolf Laban's system of movement and dance notation — can look up the rules and/or symbols of the system. However, it can also be used as a textbook by students who are unable to attend a full-time course. A two volume set, Volume 1 comprising the text and Volume 2 the examples. "This dictionary should be in the possession of all who seek to study human movement . . . No library servicing movement research and dance should be without it." *Bulletin of Physical Education*.

Illustrated

A Life for Dance
RUDOLF LABAN
Translated and annotated by
LISA ULLMANN

This new translation of Laban's reminiscences about his early life and work up to the early 1930s tells of the events, experiences and thoughts which influenced him, and contributed to his inner vision of dance. The reader cannot fail to sense the freshness and wonder of new discovery, the boundless enthusiasm for searching and experimenting in dance that filled his life at this time.

Illustrated

The Mastery of Movement
RUDOLF LABAN, *revised by* LISA ULLMANN

This standard work has been completely revised and its scope enlarged by Lisa Ullmann, who knew the changes Laban wished to make and has introduced material from his personal notes. The relationship between the inner motivations of movement and the outer functioning of the body is explored, and numerous exercises are included to challenge the student's intellectual, emotional and physical responses. The latest edition, published in large format, contains additional kinetograms, marginal annotations to act as a guide to the text, and a new appendix on the structure of effort, drawing largely on material from an unpublished book by Laban.

Illustrated

The Nature of Dance
RODERYK LANGE

This book discusses dance in the context of human culture, using the unwritten sources of dance to trace the part dance has played in the evolution of the human race. The knowledge of dance as a human faculty has until recently been limited, and the author shows clearly the importance of such a study for anyone working with dance today.

Illustrated

Personality Assessment Through Movement
MARION NORTH

This book describes a technique for personality assessment based upon Rudolf Laban's ideas about human movement. The author considers assessment and vocational guidance of children, college selection of students, work study, movement therapy and group therapy. The procedure and tests are described in detail, with many examples and suggestions for treatment.

Practical Kinetography Laban
VALERIE PRESTON-DUNLOP
This book is designed as a strictly practical introduction to Laban's system of movement notation. It has been prepared as a step-by-step guide for students and student-teachers of movement, and contains examples of notation of creative movement, dance, athletics, gymnastics and industrial activities.

Illustrated

Relaxation in Movement
DORA BULLIVANT
Perhaps more than ever before, people are seeking a more satisfactory way of life; this book provides one possible path to follow. It is the author's belief that through gentle, almost effortless movement, utilising simple and undemanding exercises, relaxation and a sense of bodily peace and well-being can be achieved.

Illustrated

Teaching Modern Educational Dance
WENDY SLATER
This book is intended for all those who have an interest in, and a basic knowledge of, modern educational dance, but who find difficulty in the presentation of their material and the planning of the lesson. For those students who are studying dance more comprehensively, the book will be useful as an additional source of creative ideas.